THE PRAYER *of* JOB

Expanded Edition—Including 46 Testimonies

Sandra Querin

Evergreen
PRESS

The Prayer of Job, Expanded Edition
by Sandra Querin
Copyright ©2002, 2004 Sandra Querin

ISBN 1-58169-145-9
For Worldwide Distribution
Printed in the U.S.A.

Evergreen Press
P.O. Box 191540 • Mobile, AL 36619
800-367-8203

TABLE OF CONTENTS

DEDICATION

I would like to dedicate *The Prayer of Job*
to my parents, Donald and Betty Hardister.

I learned how to expect a miracle and catch a vision
from my father; I learned how to persevere
until it got here from my mother.

My parents caused me to see Christ
in everything and know that I was being
held in His arms.

FOREWORD

Painful things do happen to good people. The issues of pain and suffering are among the most difficult issues of life. Disciples of Jesus often ask, "What's the point in serving God if He doesn't keep me out of harm's way? What's the point of trusting God if he doesn't prevent bad things from happening to me?"

In her book, *The Prayer of Job*, Sandi Querin takes the follower of Jesus on a soul-searching journey. Her powerful insights illustrate how God uses the difficult things of life to disclose His loving heart. To all who desire a fuller, more fruitful life: the truth contained in this book will lead you to the place beyond relationship with Christ into the place of fellowship. Peace awaits all who enter in.

Mike Bruton, Senior Pastor,
Northeast Assembly of God, Fresno, California
June 2002

INTRODUCTION

Most of us are told to be honest growing up. As time passes, we either embrace that thinking or forsake it. If we begin to walk in compromise and situational ethics, our level of honesty diminishes. Our honesty with others and with ourselves can slip to an all time low without our ever realizing it. As a general rule, our honesty before God is something we give little thought to. True honesty with God seems to have become a lost art form. We often have many truths buried so deep in us that we cannot resurrect them without the help of the Holy Spirit. We shout pain; He shouts gain!

Our God is a forgiving God, so we seek forgiveness from Him. He is a merciful God, so we enjoy His mercy. He is a long-suffering God, so we ask Him to be patient with us. He is the God of truth, but are we truthful with Him? We usually seek His blessings, but truth is more dangerous. We often find a way to run from the cemetery of our soul and the truth that lies buried there. We need to realize it is through these buried truths that the Lord can reveal Himself to us as He never has before. Honesty produces revelation.

Often, truth can be hidden because of wounds. I'm not speaking of healed wounds, I'm speaking of the wounds that would not heal—the ones we plant flowers on and call a garden. The truth cries to be delivered up, yet the wound that holds it hostage declares war on any who would come bearing a shovel. When we learn to bury truth in pain, we practice dishonesty before God. Our misunderstandings turn into disappointments, and then, left unattended, cause us to rise up in anger.

When we are honest with God, we find that we aren't nearly as bad as we thought and the Lord isn't nearly as judgmental as we thought. The enemy keeps providing seed for that garden of dishonesty, hoping that we will never dig up the truth. Hidden truth is the hidden treasure that will buy our freedom in Him. Without the honesty to find that truth, we can never fulfill our call. Without honesty, we will never really know liberty; we will always have one foot on top of that grave, lest what is buried there emerge when we're not looking.

There are reasons why God's modern day Elijahs are having trouble coming out of the cave and those of us called—as Lazarus was—won't come out of the grave. We have become like Lot because it's easier to trade our destinies in for a city of compromise. The part of us that resembles Esau dares to barter our heritage for a bowl of beans, and we're letting it happen.

Daniel said "Those who know their God will be strong and do exploits" (Dan. 11:32). Why do the exploits seem to be so far and few between nowadays? Could it be that the cave, the grave, the soup, and the cities of compromise are enough for us?

When I've become afraid of the truth, religion and tradition replace honesty. I quickly take comfort in those things and convince myself "all is well." I've figured out a system to survive and that's where my real trouble begins. It goes something like this:

As long as I don't get too close to the truth, I can't be hurt by it. Oh, I'll seek the truth all right, because that is what I've been trained to do. But, I'll escape from it just in time. I will turn and run; even act busy for Jesus, before the verse, "My God is a consuming fire (Heb. 12:29)," can affect me. I don't want to feel the heat. I will settle for relationship; fellowship costs too much. Jesus said that many are called and few are chosen. Being "called" is just fine. Why bother with being "chosen"? After all, Isaiah 48:10 says, "Behold, I have refined thee, but not with silver; I have chosen thee in the furnace of affliction." Why deliberately go into the fire? I have plenty of company right where I am.

If I just keep my walk with Christ on the surface, I won't get hurt by it. If I haven't heard what's required of me, then my lack of service or performance is no longer an issue of dishonesty, rebellion, or disobedience before God. I can't be accountable for that which I don't know."

This is a neat little system, except for one thing—it's fake and it will make us fake. It's the stuff that hypocrites are made of, and worse, it's a dishonest approach to our Christianity. King Saul and King David were both servants of the Lord. The big difference between these two men is that one was honest before God (which gave him a "heart after God's own heart"), and the other was not.

Honesty before God is a light that reflects our spirit. The Word says that "the spirit of man is the candle of the Lord." Are we keeping our candles lit? Are we brave enough or honest enough to light them? Paul told Timothy that there are vessels of honor and dishonor in the house of God. We must choose which shelf we will occupy.

Proverbs 21:16 says that if we refuse understanding, we will walk in the congregation of the dead! Where will we walk—among the living or the dead? The Word says that "signs and wonders follow those who believe." My desire is that the pages of *The Prayer of Job* will help you find the answer to this burning question, "What's following you?" It takes an honest individual to turn around and look.

CHAPTER ONE

Hope in the Midst of Trials

From the time that I committed to write this book, as the expression goes, "all hell broke loose." Somebody who lives where the sun doesn't shine was very mad! I suffered persecution and abuse on many fronts: Speaking engagements were canceled and lifetime friends abandoned me. Those who I labored over suddenly thought evil of me, cured sicknesses came to revisit me, and financial disaster came with its final blow. Oh, how I could go on and on! When we've done all to stand, then we must simply remain standing, as the Word says, especially against a contrary wind. The week that the contract came in with an offer to publish this book, like a miracle, my situation turned around. The devil had been defeated; the word would get out in spite of him. People apologized and said they "didn't know what got into them," my health returned, and God brought favor to my finances. I was living this *Prayer of Job,* and the word of God had come to "try me."

Have you ever had a wilderness experience that seemed terminal? Do you feel as if you've constantly been moving from one trial to another, and you're getting worn out?

Over the years, each time I tried to live in abundance, it slipped away from me. *Finding it* was hard enough, but *living it* seemed like an impossibility. Proverbs 21:16 says,

1

"The man that wandereth out of the way of understanding shall remain in the congregation of the dead." I didn't want to be a dead guy, so I tried my best to understand what was going on in my life, but kept failing miserably.

Every time God said great stuff was going to happen, more rotten stuff appeared. Hanging on was hard. My reality didn't seem to allow any room for faith, and my pain wouldn't let me trust. The more I paid my tithes, gave offerings, and helped and prayed for others, the sicker and more poverty stricken I became. My life was becoming a contradiction of my faith.

Constant pain from disease screamed at me from the time I was six years old but was always accompanied by the voice of God saying, "If you believe Me, I will make you well; I'll do what I say." Sometimes, what He says takes awhile to happen—with me it took 35 years. I remember being in kindergarten and grabbing my chest in pain. "Those are growing pains," I was told. *Okay, so I guess I'm going to be huge when I grow up*, I thought.

Coughing up blood, I continued to teach that Jesus delivers. Rushed to the emergency room because I couldn't breathe, I still preached healing. Left for dead, I held onto the belief that there was a work for me upon the earth.

For years, I proclaimed as Ezra did, "The hand of my God is good upon me" (Ezra 7:6), but my words only seemed to humiliate me and embarrass God. His hand felt rough and not gentle at all. I wanted to be a person who could believe even in a challenging time of unbelief, but the pain of my physical reality was growing stronger than the promise of my spiritual reality. I tried to keep myself in His hands, knowing that He was faithful to me. I learned how to fight pain and trust Christ during that time. I learned how to obey even when it looked like it was for no reason and when the world came against my obedience. I had to put my trust, not in the promise, but in the One who gave it. Eventually, I had to lay the promise down. Maybe you can't lay your promise down because you feel holding onto it is exercising your faith. When the promise we were given no longer matters, we move from *hearing* God to *seeing* Him and that's when we know the difference between faith and foolishness, that's when we touch the hem of His garment.

I had to come to the realization that He restores and renews *at His discretion and in His time*. That has to be all right. If we have learned to trust Him, it's more than all right!

Only a fervent, proven, and tried remnant of the Lord's people will trust Him and embrace liberty to forsake captivity. May we die to ourselves to be that remnant. Oh, to *see Him clearly* and not just hear Him vaguely.

True abundant living starts on the inside and manifests itself on the outside. This struggle between the spirit and the flesh has created "the walking wounded" of this current age. The walking wounded are those who have tried to have faith, tried to believe, and tried to move on, but they let the wound fester too long and the cut go too deep. The surface of the skin has healed, but the underlying tissue is infected. The walking wounded minister out of their wounds, but the Lord wants us to minister out of His healing of those wounds.

In my estimation, wounded faith is the primary cause for the lack of expectancy upon the earth today. When the disappointment is too great, we avoid the process by which it came to us. We declare, "I prayed or hoped this way or that way, and it didn't come to pass as I expected. So, I'll hold onto my knowledge and love of God, but I'm not walking down that road of expectancy again. All this faith stuff just doesn't work for me."

This is not the reason Christ died and rose again. He came so that we would be vibrant and free. He came to bestow upon us His abundance in all areas of our life, including our heart, in His way and in His time.

Fears Destroy Faith

When wounded faith opens the door to fear in our lives, it causes us to stop expecting God to fulfill His promises and undermines our trust in Him. Perfect love casts out our fears, but perfected fear destroys our faith.

In Luke 17, when Christ healed the 10 lepers, it is said that "as they went, they were cleansed." Then, one of the lepers came back, and with a loud voice glorified God, knelt down, and thanked Jesus. The Lord then said to him, "Arise, go thy way, thy faith hath made thee whole." Trust lay within his faith.

The difference between being cleansed and being made whole is huge. If you're cleansed, you can walk around without leprosy and look pretty good. But being made whole is an entirely different story. Being whole means that you are not only missing your physical leprosy, but your heart and motives are also without any kind of leprosy. Being whole will also compel you to call the leprosy out of others as you believe for their healing too. Being whole means that you trust the Lord enough to sweep the shadows out of your soul. We must forsake a mere cleansing in exchange for being made whole.

Stop planting flowers on your bondage and pretending it's a garden. That's the easy thing to do, and that's the thing we have been trained to do. The devil is counting on your love for the plantings in your soul. I had a yard like that once—lots of space and lots of weeds. One day, I got tired of looking at the weeds but was too lazy to do anything about them and too broke to hire anyone else to take care of them. So, I watered my weeds, mowed them, and called them a lawn. As long as I kept them nicely mowed and generously watered, it actually *looked like* a lawn. I even received compliments on my fake lawn. How many compliments are you getting on your "fake lawn"—the fakeness of your recovery, the fakeness of your trust in God, or the fakeness of your freedom from bondage? Our lives can be filled with so much falsehood.

When our "weeds" start to be exposed for what they really are, we have a decision to make—a critical one. Do we keep watering and mowing (I even fertilized mine from time to time), or do we go ahead, bear the expense, and put forth the effort to remove the weeds and transform our yards? Watering and mowing is what we usually do. Bondage? What bondage? Mow, mow, mow. These are not weeds; they are grass! Water, water, water. We comfort ourselves with the thought that nobody can tell the difference. But God knows the difference when He walks barefoot across your lawn. Problem is, He is always barefoot! Remember, weeds have stickers and they hurt. So, too, our fears and mistrust hurt the Lord. They hurt Him deeply.

When we decide it's time to redo our yards, sure, there is a mess, and it is expensive and inconvenient. But, if we choose Christ fully, we must stop, once and for all, watering and mowing our weeds and let Him pull them up by the roots. He knows how to get rid of those things that we have buried deep, and He does it with the least possible damage because He tenderly loves us.

Christ is the Master Gardener, and He desires our landscape to reflect who He is in us. When He has pulled up the weeds we worked so hard at preserving over the years, He plants grass that is low maintenance, allowing us to be carefree in His liberty and mercy. Isn't it time to stop pretending our weeds are beautiful? The Lord will plant and the Holy Spirit will perform the maintenance, but they are waiting for an invitation from us.

We can have faith, but without trust, it will never take us to the abundance God has for us. Sometimes we get so tired of daring to believe that things could ever be different that we just give up hoping. Maybe you have given up. The enemy of your soul will tell you that it's not worth waiting for, but the heart of Christ and, as we shall see, the story of Job will tell you that you *can* make it to the other side.

Christ doesn't look back on our troubles; He looks ahead into our triumphs. He doesn't see us as a victim but as a victor. We must decide to look forward with Christ and let Him dig up the things that keep us in bondage. Sure, re-planting our yards is messy for a little while, but when we let Him begin the remodeling of our souls, we will be forever changed and renewed. He is desperate to bless us, but He just needs us to move some things aside that are taking up space in our spirit. When we can pray the *Prayer of Job,* it will knock those things out of the way and make room for the King of Glory to come in.

What is the *Prayer of Job*? It's the prayer that emerged from Job's heart after all his trials and testings, when he at last saw his garden as God saw it. It's the prayer he prayed to judge his own impurity and come to a reckoning of his own lack. When Job's experiences taught him how to truly pray, he was no longer concerned about himself, but rather, he embraced the burden of his friends as well as his enemies.

When God commanded him to pray for his friends so that he would be set free, I believe his prayer may have gone something like this:

The Prayer of Job

*Lord, there is nothing, there is no one
who compares to You. I humble myself before You.
Search my heart and expose every motive and fear that
hinders deeper fellowship with You. Help me to trust
You through difficult trials, for they open my eyes
and heart to see You as You really are! Lord,
as for those who have come against me,
I ask You to turn Your anger from
them, forgive them, and bless
them abundantly!*

Job's prayer set him free, brought deliverance to his friends, and enabled him to walk in God's abundance for the rest of his life. When Satan was first released to test him, Job had no idea of the extent of his bondage—maybe you don't either. Job learned well the lessons of faith and trust, and you will too as you walk beside him.

CHAPTER TWO

The Greatness of the Man

There was a man in the land of Uz, whose name was Job; and that man was perfect and upright, and one that feared God and eschewed evil. His substance and household was very great...so that this man was the greatest of all the men of the East (Job 1:1-3).

To understand Job's prayer, we must first better understand the man. First of all, Job had stuff—really good stuff. The Bible tells us that Job had so much stuff that he was the greatest of all the men of the East. He had many sheep, cattle, and servants, and much land. Job also had seven sons, three daughters, and one wife. In today's language, Job had it "going on."

We know that Job was devoted to the Lord and undoubtedly held nothing higher than Him. He was also perfect, upright, God-fearing, and always stayed away from evil. He probably praised God daily as he made his sacrifices and offerings to Him saying, "Blessed be the name of the Lord" (Job 1:21). His worship stemmed out of his devotion.

However, a statement made out of *devotion* is different from one being made out of *passion* just as conviction is different than commitment—close, but still missing the mark. He needed to encounter God in a way that would forever transform his devotion into intense passion. He needed to move beyond the level of perfection he had already worked so hard to attain and hand over his deepest fears to the One who loved him.

Pursuing Perfection

Perfection is a road worth traveling. It will test and try your ability to trust the Lord. In Genesis 17:1, the Lord told Abraham to "walk before Me and be thou perfect." He didn't say, "Be perfect so that you can walk with Me." We are human; we have frailties and failings, but God figures that if we hang out with Him long enough, we'll start to look and act like He's in us. Aiming for perfection while walking with God is an ongoing process that the Holy Spirit enables us to do. It must be attainable, or the Lord would not have commanded it.

Without a doubt, Job was a good man, bent on pleasing his Maker by striving for perfection. But what God calls perfect in us is far different from what we call perfect. Above all, God is concerned with how our hearts search for Him.

Abraham's mandate to be "perfect" was a far higher call than Job's reality of it. *Strong's Concordance* describes it as being "complete and embracing truth without spot or blemish." Abraham's "perfect" was much more intense because that kind of perfection comes from walking with God and from allowing our spirits to see Him. On the other hand, the Hebrew word translated as "perfect" in the book of Job meant that he was "gentle and upright." Job was a good man, but he had not yet truly *seen* God. There is a vast different between these two concepts of perfection. Through allowing Job to suffer, the Lord would help him pursue a better definition of "perfect"—the kind that Abraham demonstrated.

Crucifying Our Flesh

The Word says that no man can see God and live. We must crucify our flesh and die to it in order to see the Lord fully, not just hear Him. We are usually so busy crying about paper cuts and fainting over a small drop of blood that we tend to put off the real surgery indefinitely.

Sometimes our human greatness stands in the way of God's greatness. We try so hard to exist with our bondages because the truth hurts and the truth costs. A woman I know is involved in a web of deceit. Her lies are ruining her life and those around her. She has forsaken her dearest friend; in fact, she almost destroyed this innocent woman. She created lies to validate and justify her position at the expense of the friend. She confessed to me that she knows she has done the wrong thing. When I asked this woman why she didn't step forward to tell the truth and set this sister free from the pain that she has caused, she replied, "The truth would cost too much. It would cost me my husband, my position at church, and the respect of my children." So, the lie reigns, and truth is forced to lay silent in her life. Her self-manufactured "greatness" has destroyed God's greatness in her.

Job's pursuit of perfection caused him to be a good person, but the deep issues of his heart were still hidden from him. I don't think he actually saw his sins until he was in the heat of battle. He figured they were just something that he would have to deal with from day to day and missed the fact that he was held captive by them.

These sins seem to start out as "nothing much"—perhaps just tendencies toward sin—but end up greatly affecting every area of our lives. They become the sins which "so easily beset us" as Hebrews 12 discusses. To survive them, we either ignore them or attempt to "pray them through." No matter how much you pray about them, until you give God permission to take them away, they're not going anywhere.

We love God, but it's the truth that sets us free, and without it, we are only imagining that we are free. Many men who commit adultery love their wives, many women who abuse their children love them, and many children who dishonor their parents love them. It's not about our feelings of love—it's about being honest and letting the love of Christ provoke us toward God's perfection.

King Saul, for example, started out as a great guy. During his reign, however, his son Jonathan accomplished heroic exploits, and Saul became jealous of him. When Jonathan killed 1,000 Philistines, Saul made the announcement that he himself killed them and had the trumpets blown and all the fanfare to celebrate the feat. If he would have refused to give in to his jealousy and instead confessed it to God when his jealousy first appeared, he could have allowed God to remove it, and his life probably would have turned out entirely different. Instead, not wanting to pay the price for a perfect walk, King Saul gave in to his jealousy, and it eventually took over his soul and destroyed him. The small bondage that crept up on him was hidden for years by his greatness—everyone had knelt before him as their king, so up till then, his jealousy had no reason to rear its ugly head. The same jealousy still tormented him 30 years later when he pursued David. He refused to let God kill it, so it killed him.

11

Trials Bring Revelation

Job probably didn't think he was in any bondage when pondering the condition of his spirit, hence the trials that God allowed in his life. Trials reveal truth, but the question is: Will we embrace that truth even if it costs us our "greatness"? If you want a new "landscape" in your heart, trials will tear up your lawn, kill the gophers, and in the process, reveal how close you are walking with the Lord, your architect.

When I was 16 years old, my father refused to allow me to go into town. Living out in the country as we did, a ride into town was always an event, and it was suddenly denied me. For about two months, he kept firmly saying "No!" when I would plead with him. I couldn't figure out the reason behind it. One day, I resigned myself to the fact that I would never go into town again, and also decided it didn't really matter. I lost my bad attitude and embraced the situation. I remember it like it was yesterday, although it happened almost 30 years ago. My dad told me something that has helped form my life. He said, "Now you can go, because you have proven that you can handle *not* going!"

When we can have a good attitude about doing without the things we earnestly desire, then we have earned the right to have them. God does not regularly take away what He has given to us, nor does He regularly test us in the way Job was tested. But, He knows the place where He wants to take us and will use whatever is available to get us there. We tend to push our character building sessions aside when the Holy Spirit tries to perfect us. Instead, by our actions, we insist on the testing.

God demanded Isaac's life from Abraham in Genesis 22:10-12, but scripture tells us that it wasn't really Isaac's life that was the issue. God was after Abraham's devotion to Isaac because He saw that it could have become greater than his love for Him. Our God is a jealous God. He does not require all of our goods and gifts, but He does require all of our *heart*.

What is your greatness? Is it standing in the way of God's purposes for you? Do you have a door in the back of the great house of your heart with an ominous sign on it that says, "I've given you everything else, but this is mine, DO NOT ENTER?"

Job found out that the only sign that really mattered was the one that gave the Lord access to it all. Before Job's trials, the difference between the perfections of Abraham and Job was as gigantic as were their hearts. The trial of Job closed the gap, but it cost him dearly. Are you willing to pay the price?

Our bondages, which can include relationships, attitudes and addictions—anything that is a substitute for our fellowship with Him—are simply closed doors with signs on them announcing how we have fallen short. The enemy contentedly smiles at them, but God likes a wide open door! True greatness is on the other side of it.

CHAPTER THREE

To Know God Is To Trust Him

Now there was a day when the sons of God came to present themselves before the Lord and Satan came also among them. And the Lord said unto Satan, Whence comest thou? Then Satan answered the Lord and said, From going to and fro in the earth and from walking up and down in it (Job 1:6-7).

God trusted Job or He wouldn't have blessed him with so very much. But Job needed to learn to trust God in the same way. Job would, in the end, come to have a mature faith built on trust. We, too, need to take our faith to this next level if we are to pray the prayer that Job prayed at the end of his trials. Unfortunately, sometimes you can only "let go and let God" when there is nothing else to do.

An old airline pilot I know tells a story of "The Last Best Hope." He says that one day he was facing the imminent crash of his plane. After all the desperate "maydays" had been broadcast and attempts to fix the situation had been made, no solution was found. Death seemed certain. After the flight attendants had given their crash instructions to the passengers, the pilot made this announcement, "All of our efforts for recovery have failed. It is my duty, according to the rules of the air, to inform you that now we must enlist 'The Last Best Hope.' Pray to God. May He have mercy on us all!" The plane didn't survive the "belly landing," but every passenger did, as well as the crew members who tell about the power of prayer.

Christ should be our *"First* Best Hope!" If we dare to trust Him, we will see the reality and proof of that in our lives. *Faith* alone says, "I believe that God heals and delivers," but *faith built on trust* says, "I believe He will do it *for me!*" The second statement is the one filled with power. Without trust, faith remains immature and lacking, always struggling to believe truly wonderful things will happen.

One spring, when my children were small, our family had a picnic on the riverbank. The children ventured out a couple feet, as they always did, because the river was famous for being shallow there. Unknown to us, the previous harsh winter had caused a shift in the currents, and the calm waters we once knew and loved were not to be trusted anymore. When I turned to unpack the picnic basket, a surge from the rapids upstream came and engulfed both my son and my daughter.

I heard them scream, and when I turned back I saw that they were already quite a distance from one another and moving fast downstream. Suddenly the tops of their heads disappeared. I heard the Lord speak to my heart: "You get her, and I'll get him," so I dove in. At first, I couldn't find Cynthia anywhere because the river was so big. Just about out of breath, I finally found her limp body at the bottom of the river and pulled her up, dragging her across the raging river, trying to keep her head above water. When we reached the river bank, Cynthia was still not breathing, but God intervened and she coughed out the water in her lungs and breath came back into her.

With all my strength gone, I struggled to stand up and look for my son. God had said He'd get Donny, but there was no sign of him. Finally, off in the distance, I saw a hand break through the water and my son came into view, climbing up on the side of a huge rock.

Later, wrapped in a towel, Donny told us how a big angel grabbed him by the shoulders and picked him up from the bottom of the river. He says that God was walking under the water playing with the fish and telling the angels what to do.

Once my daughter was safe, I must admit that my first impulse had been to jump in after Donny. I had to fight that impulse, because God said He would get him. Once we give God permission to "do something," it's no longer our business. Trust is living our faith out in real-life situations.

Psalm 20:7 proclaims, "Some trust in chariots, and some in horses: but we will remember the name of the Lord our God." To remember the name of the Lord your God is to acknowledge that He can and will do everything that is perfect for you. We must stop trying to be in control and trust Him instead.

We may have faith to believe that God created the world and all that surrounds it. We may have faith to believe that Jesus Christ is the only Son of the Living God and that He came, died, and rose from the dead. But, quite possibly, we may lack the ability to trust Him to move in *our* lives with the same power and authority. We may say, "I know Jesus walked on the water," yet not trust Him to walk through the storm that surrounds us. My grandmother used to say, "Lord, your sea is so large, and my ship is so small." Knowing that, remember that He will be in control of your ship if you'll just take your hand off the wheel and place it in His.

Giving Up Control

What's in our lives that keeps us so tangled up that we have no peace? What is it that we just can't lose control of or trust anyone with, not even Christ? Have our priorities become so scrambled that we are not only running to make ends meet financially, but also running in circles spiritually and emotionally? We need to lose control of who we have become and let Him show us who we will be.

In Judges 3:15-31, Ehud was a man who needed to trust God for a very hard and seemingly impossible thing. He could only accomplish the task God gave him by getting out of his "comfort zone." The Israelites had been in bondage to King Eglon of Moab for 18 years because of their own folly and foolishness. When they cried out for deliverance, God was merciful. He appointed Ehud—a left-handed, rock-slinging Benjamite—as their deliverer. Being left-handed, in those days, was somewhat of a handicap. And so I'm sure before Ehud became this awesome slingshot guy, he probably endured a lot of ridicule. Lots of us have, but Ehud didn't let this ridicule prevent him from becoming a man who could operate outside of his comfort zone.

If I was God, I'd have sent this guy on a rock throwing mission. But God always tries to get the most He can for us out of each opportunity. I'm sure Ehud was more comfortable with a rock and a slingshot, but instead, he used a knife. Ehud not only agreed to kill the Moabite king with a dagger but decided to craft it himself. He made a dagger, sharp on both sides, about 18 inches long. Ehud strapped the dagger onto his right thigh and journeyed to the king's palace. The guards checked his left thigh for a weapon, because that's where weapons were generally carried by the right-handed swordsmen. Finding nothing there, they allowed Ehud into the throne room to give the king a present.

17

Ehud told him that he had a secret errand for him. After everyone had left the throne room, Ehud stabbed the king with such confidence that when his dagger entered the king's belly, it was swallowed up, handle and all. Because Ehud trusted God in the middle of his own inexperience, God performed a miracle.

If we can't learn to trust, then we'll never be able to pray the *Prayer of Job*. We have to practice allowing the Lord to be in control. We have to trust Him to look out for us. To be able to pray as Job did at the end of his trial, we have to give Him our total obedience. Often, we don't mind obeying or praying, as long as we can control it. Do we pray just enough to say we did it, but not enough to get hurt by it—not enough to hear what we'd rather not hear? Many have enough faith to believe in Christ, but not enough to trust Him to work in their lives as only He can. Partial praying is really not praying at all, just as partial obedience is simply glorified disobedience. Partial praying is merely our way of attempting to control God's intentions toward us.

We must decide if we want to be a victim of our own fear and control or a product of God's will and desire.

CHAPTER FOUR

Consider Me

And the Lord said unto Satan, hast thou considered my servant Job, that there is none like him in the earth, a perfect and upright man, one that feareth God and escheweth evil? (Job 1:8).

And Job spoke of the Lord: "But, He knows the way that I take; when He hath tried me, I shall come forth as gold" (Job 23:10).

Sometimes a lengthy trial or testing is inevitable, but then sometimes it's avoidable. Many times the deciding factor is our underlying attitude. Do we have overwhelming grief in the midst of the trial, or are we steadfast in Christ? We may not be able to control our situation, but we *can* control our behavior in the midst of it.

When Job proclaims: "What is man, that Thou...dost examine him every morning and try him every moment?" (Job 7:17-18), he sounds weary and despondent. There would come a time when Job would have to reconcile his emotions with his beliefs. In other words, he would have to learn to trust God and let his emotions follow.

Many times our actions have spoken the statement, "I

know that You intend to examine me, Lord—my motives, my heart, my relationship with you—just not today." Of course, our words don't say such things—we are too accomplished at faking our spirituality. As Job embraced the examination of the Lord, so must we. When God reveals what hinders our relationship with Him, we are the ones who will need to change, not Him or anyone else.

When the devil began to demand a sifting of Job, the Lord would never have said for him to give Job his best shot if He had not trusted Job. In turn, Job would have to learn to trust God, even when He "let the dogs loose" on him.

Another man who persevered in the Lord through his trials is Joseph. Psalm 105 explains what went on with Joseph:

> *God sent a man before them, even Joseph, who was sold for a servant. Whose feet hurt with fetters; for he was laid in iron. Until the time that his word came; the Word of the Lord tried him* (Psalms 105:17-19).

You see, when the Word of God goes out on your behalf, whether it be a *rhema,* straight from God to your heart; a revelation from the Bible; a knowing, a hoping planted in you by God; or a even a prophetic utterance; it's all the same. The devil hates it and will attempt to steal it from you.

Jesus gave us a resumé of Satan when He faced him in the desert: He is a liar and a thief. He will try and cause you to disbelieve the Word, creating in you a lack of trust, and then he will come and steal the promise from you when you have taken your hands off it in dismay. The devil cannot just walk up to you and steal what has been given to you— he must be invited. Most of the time, however, we invite him without even knowing that we have done it, because we don't pay attention to what's happening around us in the spiritual realm. Ephesians 6:12 says that we must "fight principalities and powers in high places." Like it or not, we are being considered for greatness in God, so our spiritual life can't be a fragile thing. It must be tried, tested, and proven. During your process of consideration—your trial—will you fight the enemy or let him have his way? Will you hold on and trust God for the fulfillment of His promises or give up and throw them away? In whom do you have faith? In whom do you trust?

Joseph was given a fantastic word in Genesis concerning the powerful ways in which God was going to use him. Frankly, I would have kept it to myself, but he shared it with his brothers. From that moment on, his fortune went bad. His brothers sold him as a slave, and for a long time, his life was filled with one misunderstanding and trial after another.

Throughout the story, though, a strange thing is noted more than once. Just when you begin to wonder where God is, the Word says, "And the Lord was with Joseph." Right in the middle of his trouble and pain. Right in the middle of his saying, "Gee, this isn't how I remember that vision...." God was there. He is always there.

"Until the time that his word came; the Word of the Lord tried him" (Ps. 105:19). God must allow the Word He has given you to be "tried." As we have seen, Abraham was "tried" in this manner also. Many have been, and maybe you are one of them. You could be right in the middle of God's "consider this" right now. Hebrews says of Abraham, "When he was tried, he offered up Isaac." May we be willing to offer up our "Isaacs."

You see, a trial is just a "trying." Sometimes that trial doesn't seem like much because we were prepared for it.

Other times, it seems as though our lives are over. What we are doing is *trying the Word of God on for size.* Can we really handle God's Word? Is it a good fit? Will we fight the enemy for it and believe anyway?

Jude 1:3 says to "Contend for the faith." To contend means to fight for it and actually allow it to come. We must fight the enemy and trust the Lord. Will we trust the Lord through the trial without getting hung up on *what* we believed, but rather trusting *Whom* we have believed? Can it be "proven" that we believe the Lord? It was only at the end of his trial, when Job was proven, that he had the ability to pray the prayer that set him free.

When God says we're going to be rich, often we can figure on going broke first. Poverty usually runs ahead of prosperity. Sickness precedes health and persecution provides a road for peace. Not always, but often. When the saints don't understand this, they get confused and spread the confusion around to others. God's Word must always be tried and tested and proven in us.

To be well educated in the spirit and compassionate to the plight of others around us is good—a "sampler plate" of diversity at the restaurant of life. It is good to receive the "sampler," but then we must move on to the heartier fare of the dinner. Moving on to the dinner means that we correctly finished the "sampler." Aren't you tired of chasing yourself through the same ordeal over and over again? God in His mercy gives us the opportunity to "get it right."

We're supposed to "know the Lord's voice," so we will not be tricked by the schemes of the enemy. Is this current trial we're going through the will of God or a trick of the enemy? That's something that we better know! We are not meant to live in poverty or sickness, but some of us must visit there.

We should be willing to experience all the "seasons of life." God knows how long our winter will be. Trust Him for the springtime throughout the winter. The key is to not complicate it by stupid, stubborn mistakes, prolonging the arrival of the blessings that the Lord so desperately wants to bestow upon you.

For me, my sickness was a blessing. It taught me compassion that I would not have captured any other way. I am one of those folks who sees things as either black or white. Had I not spent so many years in pain, I could have easily developed the attitude that you should never be sick, ever, and if you are, you have a lack of faith or a terrible sin. Although those things are sometimes reasons for trouble, they are not the exclusive reasons, as some may say. In fact, it was far easier to be more spiritual when I was looking for my healing and being denied than after I got it! Jesus is bigger than any formula. God knows what He's doing. We have to trust Him to get the job done and not allow guilt, depression, and condemnation to overcome us while we are being "considered" in that great valley called "The Waiting."

Blessed is the man who endureth temptation: for when he has been tried, he shall receive the crown of life, which the Lord hath promised to them that love him (James 1:12).

The key to getting through a trial is to trust the One who sends you through it. We can "do all things through Christ who strengthens us" (Phil. 4:13), so if we lean on Him, we will have the strength to endure the will of God, whatever it may be. Deliverance comes. Yes, it does! Trials are fewer and farther between after the "trying" has happened, and there will come a day when the "consideration" of the desire for perfection in Him has been completed. Be blessed as you endure, for truly the trial is a privilege, as Paul calls his thorn in the flesh in 2 Corinthians 12.

Matthew Henry said, "Extraordinary afflictions are not always the punishment for extraordinary sins, but the trial of extraordinary graces. Sanctified afflictions are spiritual promotions."

Purified as Silver

And the Lord shall sit as a refiner and purifier of silver and He shall purify the sons of Levi and purge them as gold and silver, that they may offer unto the Lord an offering in righteousness. Then shall your offering be pleasant unto the Lord (Malachi 3:3-4).

A woman who had read the above passage in Malachi decided to visit a silversmith to see if she could come to a deeper understanding of it. Although not explaining the reason behind her visit, she received permission to watch the process of refining silver and ask him questions about it. "Do you actually sit there while the work of refining is going on?" she asked.

He replied, "Yes, of course I do. I must sit with my eyes steadily fixed on the furnace because if the time necessary for refining is exceeded, even in the slightest degree, the silver will be what we call injured." At once the lady saw the beauty and comfort of the expression, "He shall sit as a refiner and purifier of silver."

Before the woman left, she asked the silversmith one last question, "When do you know the process is complete?"

"That is the simplest part of all," he said. "When I can see my own image in the reflection of the silver, then the refining process is finished."

God's eyes are steadily intent on the work of purifying, and His wisdom and love are both engaged in the process. The Lord says in Isaiah 48:10, "I have refined thee, but not with silver; I have chosen thee in the furnace of affliction." May He give you the peace to trust Him as He refines you to be a chosen vessel of honor for His glory.

I would have fainted if I had not believed to see the goodness of the Lord in the land of the living. Wait upon the Lord and be of good courage, He will strengthen your heart. Wait, I say on the Lord! (Psalm 27:13-14)

Surely the "land of the living" is not a far off place.

CHAPTER FIVE

Job the Worshiper

And there was a day when his sons and his daughters were eating and drinking wine in their eldest brother's house: And there came a messenger unto Job, and said, The oxen were plowing, and the asses feeding beside them: And the Sabeans fell upon them, and took them away; yea, they have slain the servants with the edge of the sword; and I only am escaped alone to tell thee.

While he was yet speaking, there came also another, and said, The fire of God is fallen from heaven, and hath burned up the sheep, and the servants, and consumed them; and I only am escaped alone to tell thee.

While he was yet speaking, there came also another, and said, The Chaldeans made out three bands, and fell upon the camels, and have carried them away, yea, and slain the servants with the edge of the sword; and I only am escaped alone to tell thee.

While he was yet speaking, there came also another, and said, Thy sons and thy daughters were eating and drinking wine in their eldest brother's house: And, behold, there came a great wind from the wilderness, and smote the four corners of the house, and it fell upon the young men, and they are dead; and I only am escaped alone to tell thee.

Job arose and rent his mantle [tore his coat], and shaved his head and fell down upon the ground and worshiped. And said, Naked came I out of my mother's womb and naked shall I return thither: the Lord gave, and the Lord hath taken away: blessed be the name of the Lord. In all this, Job sinned not, nor charged God foolishly (Job 1:13-22).

Job began his trials with a revelation, and so he was able to continue to bless God even after losing his livestock, his servants, and his children. Make note that at this point, Job was still worshiping the Lord. Later, when he quit worshiping and began to complain about his circumstances, he lost the revelation of who God is. But if we continue to worship God in the midst of our trials, we have nothing to fear. It is in the midst of our worship that we will find the courage to pray the *Prayer of Job*.

Finding Purpose and Truth

Another Old Testament figure, Gideon, found courage as he worshiped. When the angel of the Lord called him a "mighty man of valor," Gideon discounted the description saying, "I am the least in my father's house" (Judg. 6:12). God sees the greatness in us before we do.

Gideon was afraid, but he was also obedient. He came right out and admitted his fear, so God allowed him to take a friend named Phurah along with him for security and confidence. Gideon seemed to be a weak leader, but God continued to pull him along because He had a plan. Then one day, Gideon began to worship God, and his entire world changed.

> *Gideon worshiped, and returned unto the host of Israel and said, Arise; for the Lord hath delivered into your hand the host of Midian* (Judges 7:15).

Loudly proclaiming God's deliverance, he became a strong leader and never needed to take Phurah with him again. He became a man filled with passion because he discovered God's purpose when he worshiped.

On the other hand, King Saul was somebody who had a hard time really wanting to hear the truth from God. He didn't want the truth if it was going to cost him very much.

> *Saul was afraid because of the Philistines. When Saul inquired of the Lord, the Lord answered him not, so he inquired of a witch...* (1 Samuel 28:5-8).

Fear was driving Saul into a frenzy, and when he did not get an immediate answer from the Lord, he turned to a witch. He did not inquire of the Lord for long because he figured it wasn't necessary since he had a witch hidden as a "safety net" for such a time as this.

True Inquiry

The Hebrew meaning of the word "inquire" is: "to follow, to worship, diligently seek or search out, to make inquisition with severe examination." King Saul did all those things when he inquired of the witch, but not when he inquired of God. In fact, 1 Chronicles 10:13-14 says,

*So Saul died for his transgression which he com-
mitted against the Lord, even against the word of
the Lord, which he kept not, and also for asking
counsel of one that had a familiar spirit, to enquire
of it; And enquired not of the Lord: therefore he slew
him.*

The difference between King Saul's inquiry with God
and with the witch is like the difference between running
your hand across the top of the water while at the lake and
jumping in. Both get you wet. With one you are barely in-
convenienced. With the other, you're down at the bottom of
the lake digging around. Often, at the bottom, you are cold
and lonely; sometimes, it's dark and you gasp for air. When
you come up, it takes more than a napkin to dry you off.
You did more than feel the water with your fingertips—you
emersed yourself in it. To do that, you probably changed
clothes and messed up your hairdo. The two inquiries are
that different from one another. One is an idea and the
other is an effort. One doesn't really care much about the
answer; the other *suffers* to know it.

When Saul was inquiring of God in 1 Samuel, he was
faking it (mowing weeds) because God's answer was not
something that he diligently sought. However when he inquired of the witch, he paid a heavy price for it by breaking
the Hebrew law and risking God's wrath. So this, indeed,
was true inquiry. In reality, he had also worshiped the witch
because it's a form of worship when we go to seek the truth.

When our answers don't immediately come, what will we
do—seek God or find a witch? If we trust God, we can wait
for His answer.

I had been in and out of the hospital on numerous occa-
sions with serious problems due to my disease. The final

time I was there, they had taken medical tests, blood gases, and did a variety of fun things like probing my veins, before I was sent home. Evidently, on their seventh or eighth try to get my blood, they had punctured something, and unbeknownst to anyone, I began to bleed internally. After a couple days at home, I felt strange so I called the doctor. After hearing my symptoms, he deemed it somewhat of an emergency and told me to meet him at the hospital in an hour. He told me that under no circumstances should I wait even a moment if I started to get "lighting bolt, jerking pains" in my arm. That would indicate that it was worse than he thought, and that there was a possibility that I could very quickly lose not only my arm, but even my life.

I was pretty well convinced that a nap would probably solve my problem, so I laid down to get a little rest, thinking that it was all going to go away. Suddenly I got those "jerking pains" the doctor had warned me about. I prayed, but the jerking pains continued. I received no direction from the Lord, so I got ready to leave for the hospital. As I was putting my shoes on, I became overwhelmed with gratitude that it was not my right arm that I was going to lose. I couldn't get over the generosity of God because learning how to function left-handed would have really irritated me. I begin to praise Him for this and then got lost in worshiping His greatness. Tears of joy for the privilege of serving Christ began flowing down my face. It was a great moment, and I wish I could say that I have always lived there.

During this time of worship, I became excited about the next adventure and had confidence that He would not leave me alone in it. I dried my face and told myself, "Well, let's go get my arm cut off and see what will grow in its place!" But then something happened. I noticed that my fingers were no longer plastered together. They had been so swollen before, they had looked like black balloons. Soon the swelling was entirely gone out of my arm and shoulder and the blackness of the skin from the internal bleeding turned to normal color. Within about five minutes, I had a complete healing of my arm! It was when I lost myself in worshiping God that everything that was not of Him disappeared.

Find a way to be a worshiper. The best way is to be still. God says in Psalms 46:10: "Be still, and know that I am God: I will be exalted among the heathen, I will be exalted in the earth."

"Be still and know that I am God." Could that mean that if we are not still, we won't know Him? Sometimes we get so busy chasing God around that we forget to slow down long enough to let Him catch us. He is in hot pursuit of us in this game of life that we play, so let Him win. Be still.

CHAPTER SIX

Losing Greatness

So went Satan forth from the presence of the Lord and smote Job with sore boils from the sole of his foot unto his crown. Job took a potsherd to scrape himself withal; and he sat down among the ashes. Then said his wife unto him, Dost thou still retain thy integrity? Curse God and die! (Job 2:7-9)

Now, on top of everything else, Job sat in a pile of ash and scraped his body because boils had formed from the top of his head to the bottom of his feet. Then, to make matters worse, his nagging wife added to his affliction. I guess maybe she wanted him dead, or perhaps she had been publicly humiliated by his situation or taunted by the other women and couldn't handle it. At this point, you may be asking, "Why didn't God set the hell hounds loose on her?" God doesn't operate like that.

Much to Job's credit, when his wife berated him for keeping his integrity, he replied, "The Lord gave and the Lord hath taken away; blessed be the name of the Lord" (Job 1:21). This statement is birthed out of the revelation Job had as a worshiper.

The Lord is waiting for us to be willing to trust Him and

forsake our fears. Fear will destroy God's work in us and cause us to be missing spiritual body parts and become deformed like a spiritual accident.

Past Greatness

Job reflected on his past greatness in Chapter 29. He began with regrets that the "good old days" were gone. "God used to preserve and protect me. It was great when God was with me and my children were about me. I had so much money that I used to wash my steps with butter and rivers of oil flowed on my land. Old men would stand up when I came into the room, and young men would hide. I had power and position and prosperity. Even royalty stopped talking when I came in the room. I helped all the sick, lonely, and poor people. I had a ministry. I was the eyes of the blind and feet to the lame. I stood against evil and fought for justice. People always heard my counsel and sought me out for it. I was like a chief, a king in the army" (author's paraphrase). That's a lot of greatness.

In verse 3, Job refers to the God of his yesterdays: "When His candle shined upon my head." If God's candle is shining upon your head, your own spirit is revealing truth, even when you are not looking. This is what happened to Job. The Holy Spirit was searching Job's soul with the help of his own spirit. This is the problem with getting just enough of God to appear righteous. It's dangerous because you have agreed with God, and from that moment on, your spirit is longing to join together with the rest of you—your body and soul as one—to worship your Maker. Your spirit groans to come into that unity.

When you said, "I do" to Jesus, you proclaimed that you would become one with Him. Your own spirit is shining on the areas in your life that are not pleasing to the Lord and asking for a way to clean things up. The only concern of loss we should have is David's plea in Psalm 51:11, "Cast me not away from thy presence; and take not thy holy spirit from me."

No matter how great our ministry, testimony, or calling, God is after the perfection of our hearts. He cares more about who we are than what we can do for Him. Sometimes we can get so wrapped up in "doing" that we ignore the condition of our own hearts and lose the presence of the Lord. It's a cheap insurance policy that will never pay off; we think we're covered by our actions, but we're not. God is after the the intent of our souls, not so He'll discover the truth about us (because He already knows it), but so that *we'll* know and modify the reason behind our actions.

We need to walk in honesty and not deception. That's why scripture says, "Seek ye first the kingdom of God and His righteousness and all these other things will be added unto you" (Matt. 6:33). The words that Jesus spoke will come to pass one day when it's all over: "Many will say, Lord, Lord, we cast out demons in your name, healed the sick in your name.....the Lord will say, depart from me you workers of iniquity, I know you not" (Matt. 7:23). The intent of our souls and the condition of our hearts become of utmost significance in the light of these scriptures. The only thing we should refuse to lose is our walk with the Lord. That is not up for grabs, but everything else needs to be. We must be willing to lose our greatness to make room for His greatness!

God's Habitation

When we accepted Jesus as the Lord of our lives, He began to dwell in our spirits, but the condition of our souls, bodies, and minds are still up to us.

And be not conformed to this world: but be ye trans-formed by the renewing of your mind, that ye may prove what is that good, and acceptable, and perfect, will of God (Rom. 12:2).

How will we behave? What about our attitudes, wills, and desires? When we accepted Jesus as Lord, it didn't mean we would be robots or even "godbots." What it meant was that we gave Jesus permission to be Lord and also gave Him permission to help us act like it.

God will not take our will away, and that's a problem for us most of the time. That's why there are so many "saved people" out there who talk the talk but just can't live the life or walk the walk. They want to, but not badly enough to forsake anything else to get there. They are eternally struggling and slipping around, sliding from one "I'm gonna" to the next. Is that you? Has the Lord entered your spirit, but are the other three corners of your being—your body, mind, and soul—filled with so many things that there is no room for Him?

When we receive Christ, He takes up residence in our spirit and heart. He expects us to renew our minds by reading the Word and wants us to be "holy in all manner of conversation" (1 Peter 1:15). The Lord has done the hard part by saving us from eternal destruction. But how do we live a sanctified life? None of us is righteous, pure, holy, or perfect, but the Lord has told us to make an attempt with His help at a better way by using His overcoming and conquering power that allows us to be more than conquerors.

With Christ in my spirit, I am saved from hell but not from myself. I have to work at that by willingly giving over my whole being to the Lord. I gave the Lord my spirit, but what about my mind, body, and soul which includes my intellect, desires and will? If I refuse to walk differently than I did in the past, Christ will only remain in my spirit, and I will struggle with my Christianity. But if I go forward by joining in godly fellowship, reading the Word, and worshipping, then my intellect will become altered toward God, and my desires and decisions will be more godly. I will begin to *want* to do what is right, and before long, it will be natural for me to act as Jesus would act in any given situation. If we are not acting as Jesus would, then we haven't given our whole self over to Him. If we don't look toward Jesus after we know Him, we will never look like Him. We will have a formal relationship with Him but not fellowship. We will say that we are a Christian, but we will never look like one because the walk will be too hard. So many times the world is looking at Christians, hoping that they will live what they believe, for if the Lord can't change us, how could He change them?

Someone came to me with a problem they couldn't overcome—an involvement with pornography. He was a pastor and was about to lose everything. We prayed and he was set free from it. Two weeks later, he began to fall back into it, and I asked him if he was reading the Word. He said that he was. I told him that he wasn't reading enough because he had been delivered and the bad spirits were gone. The only thing that could pull him back into the sin now was himself. He was the only one who had the ability to lose the power of God in his life. He didn't make right choices because he forgot he was in a war for his soul. His spirit belonged to Jesus, but his mind, body, and soul belonged to him. Until he handed these over to God, things wouldn't change. Although he was reading the Word every day, obviously it wasn't enough. He was sick and the Word was his medicine. So he tripled the reading time and his whole being became flooded with the thoughts and intentions of God, and he lost himself to fully gain Christ. He had to cancel his appointments for awhile. I told him he was sick and needed to radically separate himself from everything to gain his spiritual strength.

The devil doesn't like to lose, and he is a fighter. The Lord is greater, but we have to more than give Him permission to change us—we have to get out of the way. Within a few short days, the pastor was transformed. He began to fight the evil that was trying to destroy him, and through Christ, he won the battle! It's a beautiful thing to see him pray for other people now. To see the pure love of God emerge from him is a true testimony of what kind of power God has in our lives, when we "let go and let God."

The more of Jesus that we allow in our spirit, the more of Jesus there will be to flow over into our mind. The more of Jesus that we allow in our mind, the more of Jesus there will be to flow over into our body. The more of Jesus we have in our body, the more of Jesus there will be to flow over into our soul. He gets bigger and bigger if we allow Him to and eventually our desire will be as it was for Paul, "And to know the love of Christ, which passeth knowledge, that ye might be filled with all the fullness of God" (Eph. 9:13). So basically, the question is, Do we want a lot of Jesus or a little bit? It is entirely up to us.

First John 1:5 says, "God is light, and in him is no darkness at all." When the Lord is in your spirit, He brings light—joy, peace, hope, and salvation. He sweeps the darkness out of our spirit. But He expects us to give Him the other three corners of our being: our mind, body, and soul. There can be much evil locked up in those areas that goes untouched for years, even though we are a Christian and truly love Jesus. Our struggles stem from loving Jesus, but not giving Him complete access to our lives. For example, we may love Jesus, but just can't quit getting drunk, or cut our bad friends off, or stop using drugs. That's when we love Jesus, but.... However, when we give Him all our being, then all of a sudden, "He's enough!"

Sometimes, it's a matter of salvation and sometimes a matter of deliverance. As it says in 2 Corinthians 6:2, "Behold, now is the day of salvation" and Luke 4:8 says He has come "to preach deliverance to the captives." They are surely different things. The Lord will deliver us of all that ails us, but then we must determine to follow Him with our whole being. If we don't, Hebrews 10:29 says, "Of how much sorer punishment, suppose ye, shall he be thought worthy, who hath trodden under foot the Son of God, and hath counted the blood of the covenant, wherewith he was sanctified, an unholy thing, and hath done despite unto the Spirit of grace?"

It is His pleasure to give us our own free will and the ability to choose how awesome of a Christian we will be by determining how much of ourselves we will yield to Him. That yielding or submission determines the depth of our devotion and fellowship with Him.

The more we allow the Lord to be in our spirits by reading of the Word, by worshipping, by deliberately making right choices no matter how difficult they are, and by drawing close to Him, the more we are "opening the doors" to our mind, body, and soul so that He can reside there as well. (In the same way we open those doors to evil when we don't draw close to Him.) When these four corners of our being—spirit, mind, body, and soul—are filled with the Lord, we are a sanctified being. Does that mean we are perfect? No! It simply means that the devil can't get us as he used to do, and we are not tempted in the same way we used to be tempted. At that point, we are walking in power and not fear or selfishness; we are doing more learning and rejoicing than struggling.

If we love Jesus but just can't seem to live a holy life, then perhaps we have neglected to give Him the other parts of our being as well as our spirit. For example, watching perverted or unedifying movies or keeping company that offends the Lord, takes back our permission for Him to enter into our mind, body, and soul. Sometimes people forever have a craving because their bodies have not submitted to the Lord, or they cannot be rid of bad thoughts because they have not given their mind to Christ and don't have His mind in exchange. (A generation that is in constant need of entertainment often doesn't use much discretion about what kind of entertainment they get. They just don't want to have to think, and that is the devil's playground. *The Prayer of Job* will never be prayed from that place.)

Sometimes people just can't determine to make the right choices because there is not enough of Jesus in them to be spread around into the other areas of their being beyond the spirit. Jesus will help us make the right choices, but we have to be submitted to Him and agree to be led by the spirit and not by our own fleshly desires and thoughts.

The Lord, of course, can handle us, but the problem is that we have to *allow* Him to do so, and so often we don't. We get so busy justifying why we can do something that we forget to ask ourselves the question, "Why would I want to?" All things are available, but not all things are necessary. You see, Jesus doesn't remain outside when you go into the bar; He doesn't run away when you listen to a bad joke; He doesn't hide in the bathroom when you are watching an inappropriate movie—He is sitting right there with you. He said He would never leave you nor forsake you, and He won't!

The Lord asks the question in the Word, "Where is the habitation that you have built for me, for God dwells in men." A dirty habitation will not please the Lord. Oh, He'll come there, but His power and anointing cannot rest there. The Holy Spirit won't allow it. So, we make the critical decision about our spiritual destiny. The Lord is waiting, but who will prepare the place for Him in their lives? The Word says that "The eyes of the Lord run to and fro throughout the whole earth, to show Himself strong on behalf of them whose heart is perfect toward Him" (2 Chr. 16:9). The "perfect" here means one who is ready, whole and full. Would that be you?

Paying the Price

Most of the signers of the Declaration of Independence eventually lost everything they had—finances, favor, friends, and family. These 56 men made an oath to something larger than themselves, giving up everything in order to form what we now enjoy as the great United States of America. Sometimes losing everything is the only option. We must weigh the cost and then pursue it with a vengeance as they did when they stood straight and unwavering while they pledged:

> For the support of this declaration, with firm reliance on the protection of the divine providence, we mutually pledge to each other, our lives, our fortunes and our sacred honor.

As it turned out, everything they offered was required of them. Many of their wives were murdered and children imprisoned. They were left penniless and wounded, but still they would not relent. They kept their eyes on where they were going and trusted God to get them there. And He did.

It is said of Thomas Nelson, Jr., that during the Battle of Yorktown in the Revolutionary War, British General Cornwallis had taken over his home and was using it as his headquarters. Thomas urged General George Washington to open fire. General Washington at first refused, for it was believed that Nelson's family was also being held captive inside. With tears in his eyes, Mr. Nelson quietly urged General Washington to open fire, for he had made a solemn pledge.

When General Washington reluctantly gave the command, the home was destroyed and no one survived. The destruction of the enemy's headquarters became the turning point of the war. Thomas Nelson, Jr. died alone and bankrupt. What a price he paid to fulfill his vow. He had no fear, only passion and purpose. Such are the stories of the American Revolution. Those people had security, but valued liberty more. What have you held onto in your soul all these years that you are now willing to risk for true spiritual liberty?

Paul's Transformation

Saul of Tarsus was the son of a Pharisee. He had position, prosperity and power. He was trained by Gamaliel, the "Billy Graham" of his day. He also had a second occupation, according to Jewish tradition, as a maker of tents. Even this second occupation was prestigious. The goats that roamed on the hills of Tarsus were known for their beautiful hair. It needed to be skillfully woven in a particular fashion to be strong and sturdy, and Saul of Tarsus knew how to do it.

Out of the 6,000 men allowed to operate in the office of a Pharisee at any one time, only 70 of them were part of the high council called the Sanhedrin, and Saul of Tarsus was one of them. He had the king's ring on his finger, so his word and command were second only to the king himself. Saul of Tarsus was a defender of righteousness, and he went about defending God from the Christians, imprisoning them, and seeing to their persecution or death.

One day, while heading toward Damascus, Saul was given a revelation that Jesus Christ is truly the Son of God and gave up everything to embrace it. God changed his name to Paul as he entered in his new occupation as an advocate for Christ. He was still hated and feared by many Christians because of his prior persecution of them, and his old bosses in the Roman Empire even tried to kill him. He suffered immensely, but counted it a privilege. In fact, toward the end of his life, while he was writing to the Philippians as an imprisoned old man, he said, "Oh that I might know Him and the power of His resurrection, and the fellowship of His sufferings, being made conformable to His death" (Phil. 3:10). Relationship wasn't enough; he was seeking the perfection of his fellowship with Jesus up to the very end.

The devil couldn't get to Paul of Tarsus because there was nothing to get. Paul had already given it all to the Lord and moved in phenomenal power and authority. We cry out for that power, but when the going gets tough, we usually consider the price too high.

A man by the name of James Calvert went to be a missionary to the Fiji Islands many years ago. The captain of the ship that delivered him to the destination of his calling didn't want to leave him. He said that he'd be back in a few days to pick James up because he'd surely want to leave. The captain told him that the people on the islands were cannibals, and they would more than likely kill him. Mr. Calvert would hear none of it and kept packing his things to go on shore. As Mr. Calvert was walking away into the dense forest to meet his destiny, the Captain shouted to him, "Mr. Calvert, please come back; you will die if I leave you." Mr.

Calvert turned around, spread out his arms, smiled and shouted back. "I died before I came!" He caused a great revolution for the gospel in his day. Where is our revolution?

CHAPTER SEVEN

When Fear Destroys Faith

For the thing which I greatly feared is come upon me and that which I was afraid of is come unto me (Job 3:25).

To fear God is to understand who He is and to respect Him. If we fear anything or anyone else, it proves we do not trust God to be who He says He is.

Somehow, the only way for God to merge His greatness with Job's was to use the enemy to bring his fears to the surface. If all we can do is worry about what we will lose, then it shows us that our hearts are in the wrong place. Does this mean that the only way to be great in God is to lose everything? Of course not. But it does mean that if we declare before the Lord that we want to walk with Him in fellowship and see Him, then everything is up for grabs. The Lord will stop at nothing to answer our prayer for intimacy with Him. We have to trust Him to accomplish it in whatever way He sees fit.

Psalm 42:7 says, "Deep calleth unto deep." That is our soul calling to God, "Cause me to know You as I am known by You." There is no room for bondage in that yearning, nor is there room to fear a loss.

Job thought he trusted the Lord, but here we find an element that destroyed his trust—fear. Fear is the opposite of faith, and it wars against trust. Our fear of losing something can't be larger than our trust of the Lord with it.

In the midst of the fervor and favor of his former life, Job harbored fear deep down in his soul. *Fear will provoke us to react on our own.* Jonah fearfully ran to the sea and turned his back on his call to prophesy to the people of Nineveh. *Fear will provoke us to become impatient.* King Saul's impatience in calling upon the witch lost him his kingdom. *Fear will provoke us to hide our faces from God.* At the burning bush, Moses shrank back from God. It was only after his revelation of who God really is and what He wanted that Moses was able to face God and trust Him for the challenges of leading His people. *Fear will provoke us to be dishonest before God because honesty requires bravery.* Fear of a few giants caused the Israelites to wander in the desert for 40 years.

Fear can cripple you and hold you captive against your will. Fear can own you if you let it. Fear is one of the hardest things to get rid of because, beyond the spiritual implications, there are very real emotional and physical reactions to it as well. Fear can crush you, but trust will encourage you. We must commit to destroy our fear in order to empower our trust.

While I was waiting for my healing from cystic fibrosis, things called bronchiectasis and emphysema were adding misery to my horror. I was told I needed surgery to remove the lower part of my left lung. Recovery would be difficult, and there were many possible complications. "I'd rather not," I told the Lord. "Just zap me. You've supernaturally healed me of all these other things—just go for my lung now, surely it's time for you to visit my disease." Thus I began my negotiation with the Almighty. "All you'd have to do is sneeze or just wave your hand..." He wasn't getting it. For some reason, the Lord was immovable.

He showed me that the reason I wanted to be healed so badly wasn't for the glory of God and wasn't because I knew I was bought by the Blood with certain inherited rights. It was because I had a fear of surgery. I survived the surgery to trust the Lord more than I ever had, and supernatural healing of all that ailed me came soon enough afterwards. Receiving my healing too early in this would have stunted my spiritual growth and accommodated my fear, so for 35 years, I waited in pain and survived against all natural odds.

Job had a fear of losing everything, so he prayed continually to insure that it wouldn't happen. When he says "the thing I greatly feared has come upon me," he is speaking in panic. He had a fear of losing something, so he tried to use his prayers and tears in place of trusting God.

Fears can frustrate and complicate our faith, preventing us from truly trusting God. We sometimes use the semblance of spiritual things to hide the truth, so that we won't have to face the fears that are hidden within our faith. As the Word says, "Having a form of godliness, but denying the power thereof" (2 Tim. 3:5). We often perform just enough to "be in the club," but never enough to trust the One who invited us in. Some people, I suppose, have enough of God to be miserable in a bar, but not enough to be happy in a prayer meeting.

Trusting God

Throughout the book, Job's fear is exposed. Job pleads, "Let God take away His rod from me and let not His fear terrify me. Then I would speak, and not fear Him, but it is not so with me" (Job 9:34-35). Job does much talking *about* God and *at* God, but little directly *to* Him at this point. He would discover that life is not about *our* performance, it's about our ability to trust *His* performance.

When the army of Israel stood before Goliath after his "invitation" to a fight, it is recorded that "they were dismayed and greatly afraid. And all the men of Israel, when they saw the man, fled from him and were sore afraid" (1 Samuel 17:24). Their fear destroyed their testimony. We know this is true because when Goliath demanded that the Israelites choose a worthy opponent for him in verse eight, he addressed them as, "You servants of Saul." He did not call them servants of God, but merely servants of King Saul. That was definitely a cutting remark. We can't let our fears rewrite our testimonies.

Fear is such a strong spirit that it will attempt to consume and destroy anyone in its path—your family, friends, and co-workers. It manifests itself in a variety of ways in different people. It is uncontrollable and aggressive—definitely not a toy. The best way to handle fear is to commit yourself to get rid of it. Ask God to remove it and practice living without it. Modify your behavior and be full of the Word. Paul told Timothy to "exercise godliness." I get tired of people saying that God just didn't "lift the sin" from them; or they have "no desire" to read the Word, so they don't; or that "God made me this way," which is a classic excuse for wrong behavior. Are you saying those things? God is holding His hand out to take them from us, but we must reach out toward Him.

I believe in miracles, probably more than most, since I'm living one, but a miracle doesn't change your character. It makes you feel better, but it doesn't change who you are. It may change *what* you are, but not *who*. Expect and believe for great and mighty things. But, when the great and mighty things happen to come in the form of a "still small voice" speaking in your soul, be sure to listen and respond to Him.

I used to have such a horrible fear of spiders—arachnophobia, they call it—that it would paralyze me at times. When I had children, they started to mimic me and act out their "learned fear." That was enough for me. I prayed and prayed, but God would not supernaturally deliver me from this horror the way I desired. So, I took my prayer, gave it feet, and put it into motion. I knew the Lord would help me, but He wanted me to participate. I had my husband catch a "muscle builder" spider with hair all over it and put it into a jar. It was a huge spider. If I so much as touched the jar, I would start to shake. So, I put the jar on the counter and covered it up with a towel. A few times a day, I would lift the towel and look at the spider. I slowly progressed to the point that I didn't need the towel anymore. I eventually started carrying the jar around.

I carried that jar with those tiny air holes in the top around with me until the spider died. Then we got another one. This went on for about a month. I gave myself a time limit because fear should have a deadline. At the end of that month, I opened the jar myself and killed that spider, and I've been killing them ever since!

Kill yours, so that you can get on with abundant living. What holds you hostage? Whatever it is, I promise you, it is eating away at your faith and destroying your ability to trust the One who made you in His image. There's no more time to waste babysitting fear. Fear will prevent you from being honest with God and praying Job's prayer.

The Spirit of our God is roaming across this earth performing exploits for His glory, and He wants us to be part of it. It is not a fearful work; it is a work of power. Let's not miss it! Many followers of Jesus missed it because they were afraid to pay the cost to follow Him. They assumed the price would be too great. In reality, the cost is higher when we hold onto fear and deny the Lord. Whatever our quest or our call, and wherever it may be—at home, the office, church, or grocery store—we must be free to embrace the price that leads to freedom.

I found out what makes a hero: Someone who is willing to be brave for five minutes longer than anyone else! Let's be heroes today and trade our fears in for faith.

CHAPTER EIGHT

When Grief Is Greater Than Grace

And when they [his friends] lifted up their eyes afar off, and knew him not, they lifted up their voice and wept and they rent everyone his mantle and sprinkled dust upon their heads toward heaven. So, they sat down with him upon the ground seven days and seven nights and none spake a word unto him, for they saw that his grief was very great (Job 2:12-13).

The one thing that we have to realize about Job's friends is that they started out as great guys. Although tradition tells us that these three were Job's bad and horrible friends, that's not how they began. The above verses tell us that they actually made an appointment together to come and visit their friend in his time of pain and sorrow.

Job's friends recognized his fear. In Job 11:15 and 19, his friend, Zophar, made the following statement to encourage him: "You will lift up your face without spot, yea, thou shalt be steadfast and shalt not fear. You will lie down and none shall make thee afraid" (Job 11:15). One of the definitions of Abraham's "perfect" was "without spot," the same phrase that Zophar used. Zophar pointed out what Job could become and told his friend to get rid of his fear so that he could enjoy what God had next for him.

Zophar is telling Job, "You don't have to live in fear and have 'minor perfection.' You can have 'major perfection,' the kind that Abraham had, with no blemishes upon it." He is saying, "Let the attributes of God perfect you and take away your fear so that you are without spot or wrinkle."

Job's friends continued to try and salvage him by calling out his fear and speaking prophetically to him of great things ahead. In Chapter 5 they said, "You will be hid from the scourge of the tongue, neither shalt thou be afraid of destruction when it comes. At destruction and famine, you shall laugh, neither shall thou be afraid of the beasts of the earth." In other words, they were saying, "Don't worry Job, there's coming a day when you won't be afraid any more."

They continued to tell him he would enjoy a prosperous and long life, "Thou shalt come to thy grave in a full age" (Job 5:26). They told him that his past was going to seem like small potatoes compared to the great thing that God had for him. They told him he would laugh and rejoice again and pronounced that he was a good man.

At first they worked fervently to help Job remove his fear, but he wasn't ready to change yet. Before long, they were singing Job's song because they were influenced by his negative attitude and were not strong enough to fight it. Let's remember that for seven days and nights they were together, and no one spoke. His friends mourned with him and genuinely felt badly. When someone finally spoke in Chapter 3, it was Job, full of dismay and cursing the day he was born. He spread grief to his friends in the middle of his pain and didn't let up until it consumed them too. At this point they become the "bad friends" we all have come to disparage, and the Lord eventually rebuked them severely. By the end of their discussions, Job was worse off and so were his friends. They lost sight of God and twisted both Job's words and God's intent. They began to pervert judgment in the name of the Lord. They spoke enough truth to appear sound in faith but bathed it in hypocrisy and evil.

Perfect Peace

The Word says that Job's "grief was very great." If your grief is very great, maybe your mind has wandered into the quagmire of your situation and out of His promise. Maybe your trouble has consumed your trust. Where there is fear, there is no peace.

In Isaiah 26:3-4, the Lord says, "I will give him perfect peace whose mind is stayed upon me, because he trusts in me. Trust in the Lord forever." Perfect peace leaves no room for fear. Perfect peace comes from fixing our minds on Him because we know His Word, and we know Him. Perfect peace comes from finding a place deeper than we are. Perfect peace comes from the Lord Himself. Forget *what* you know; it's *who* you know that counts—the One who still walks upon the troubled waters that surround us.

The books of Jeremiah and Lamentations are some of the most powerful in the Bible. They contain some of the most comforting and profound promises we will ever have the privilege of depositing into our souls. The reason? They were birthed out of the writers' great grief, pain, and perseverance.

Nothing of great value is regularly obtained without a degree of pain and sorrow. Pain and sorrow do not last forever, but while they are with us, let's rejoice in them, knowing that they are paving the way for our greatness in God, something that will last forever.

Jeremiah was the weeping prophet. He was thrown into the dungeon, beaten, mocked, imprisoned, and more. All of this happened because he wouldn't be quiet about God's plan for His people. Even when they wanted to listen, they struck him when he spoke. He couldn't win coming or going. God asked him to do hard things in the face of an unfriendly nation. Before Jeremiah ever left on his mission, God warned him, "They shall fight against thee, but they shall not prevail against thee, for I am with thee, saith the Lord, to deliver thee" (Jer. 1:19).

At one point, Jeremiah hit a low spot and decided that he had done enough. Up until then, his prophecies to the people had only resulted in his being thrown into jail. None of the them had yet been fulfilled. Jeremiah announced that he was not going to talk about the Lord anymore or prophesy in His name.

However, Jeremiah didn't let his personal pain stand in the way of his presentation of God's message for long. The beautiful thing about Jeremiah is that in the next breath, he said, "But His word was in mine heart as a burning fire shut up in my bones, and I was weary with forbearing, and I could not stay." Jeremiah was saying here, "I can't help myself. My call is in my bones. I'm more miserable disobeying God. I can't stay like this. I can't ignore my purpose. I don't care what it costs, but it can't be worse than this fire in my bones." He recovered quickly from his despondency and so should we.

Functioning in God's Power

Moving to a modern day example, let's look at a woman named Ellie, who also knows how to function in the power of God. When her son was violently murdered, she gave herself a couple days to grieve. Then, she rose up and worshiped her God and praised Jesus night and day that her son was with Him in glory. She glorified God right through her grief and began to worship Him in the middle of the situation and pray for the murderer. Only the Holy Spirit can inspire that kind of prayer, and that's the kind He's trying to inspire in us today. The joy she gained was supernatural. She had unwavering peace in a time of great grief. Ellie believed Romans 8:28 and magnified her Savior right to the other side of her sorrow. She trusted the Lord for the fulfillment of this scripture in her life. "We know that all things work together for good to those who love God, to those who are the called according to His purpose."

The young man who murdered her son found Christ in prison because of Ellie's prayers and has now become in her words, "like a son." As it turned out, he had no family of his own and was a product of the streets. He now has a family, and sweet restoration was given to him because someone was willing to enlist Job's prayer for his benefit and God's glory.

Isaiah 42:3 says that "A bruised reed shall he not break," so God will not give us more than we can bear. We must trust God to know what we can bear—His perceptions, not ours; His reality and timing, not ours. If your "grief is so great," remember, so also is His grace! But if our grief has become greater than God's grace, maybe we don't understand what grace is. Grace is our ability to walk in Christ with power and authority over all things, including our grief. Grace is what Calvary left behind and what the resurrection secured. Never allow anything to become greater than grace. Grace allows us to walk in our full inheritance.

Isaiah 53:3-4 speaks of Jesus:

> *He is despised and rejected of men; a man of sorrows and acquainted with grief: and we hid as it were our faces from Him. He was despised and we esteemed Him not. Surely He hath borne our griefs and carried our sorrows.*

In 1 Peter 2:19 it says, "For this is thankworthy, if a man for conscience toward God endure grief, suffers wrongfully." Even if you don't have it coming, especially if you don't have it coming, endure and trust Him to make your trial worth something in the end. He is faithful to bring you through.

CHAPTER NINE

Is Your Righteousness Bigger Than God's?

So these three men ceased to answer Job, because he was righteous in his own eyes (Job 32:1).

Job's friends were not seeing the Lord in Job anymore because he was no longer the worshiper he used to be. Self-righteousness will cause us to defend ourselves and not allow us to see, no matter how small, any reason why we could be wrong. In that situation, small fears cannot be detected and therefore lay hidden within the confines of self-righteousness and false humility. It isn't that we don't care for others, but that we care more about protecting ourselves than wanting to be exposed. The blanket of who we pretend to be covers us up nicely.

When we are covered by that blanket, truth won't abide in us and neither will Christ's power and authority. We cry for power, but oftentimes we cry louder for physical deliverance than for spiritual understanding. Why do we force God to get out the jack hammer?

Temptations Abound

Hezekiah was a great king. In fact, he was an all around

great guy. The Word says that he did "that which was right in the sight of the Lord." It's almost a miracle when you consider the example that he had. His father, King Ahaz, was mad at God, and the more distress he was in, the more he sinned. He refused to come to God even in his time of trouble. He was so ticked off at God that he started to worship the false gods of the people who whipped him in battle, just to make God angry. Hezekiah's father tore up the house of God, burned the things used for worship, and barred the doors. He deliberately provoked God to anger. He was such a rotten guy that when he died, they wouldn't even bury him with the other kings.

Hezekiah became king when he was 25 years old and reigned for 29 years. We have to assume that he had godly teachers and a mother with a positive influence on him since she was the daughter of Zechariah (2 Ch. 29:1). He was gifted, talented, well-liked, passionate, kind, healthy, and wealthy. God gave him "exceeding much riches and honor....storehouses and cities to hold all his abundance, for God had given him substance, very much" (2 Chr. 32:27,29). He had entire cities just to store his "stuff." We are told that Hezekiah prospered in all his works. He brought water in and created rivers. He is responsible for the hanging gardens, which were considered a "wonder of the world" in his time. God helped him to achieve impossible things.

He was a brilliant individual who loved God with all his heart and sought Him for His will and the direction of His people. He saw to it that Israel brought in the abundance of their first fruits for the tithe and also gave offerings. He created a call of purity that was heard throughout the land, and he was valiant in war. He got up early in the morning and made his leaders do the same so they could accompany him to seek God for the day. He was a tremendous leader and manager. He saw to it that the house of God was repaired and restored. He edified the priests in their duties and not only encouraged holiness, he demanded it. He went to great lengths to remove the curse that his father had placed upon the nation. Hezekiah was a good and trustworthy king. He did not seem to have any hidden sins.

Whatever he did for the Lord, he did it "with all his heart and prospered." He did that which was "good, right and truthful before the Lord." He prepared the people to seek God like they hadn't done for years. There hadn't been so much joy in Jerusalem since the time of Solomon, and there had never been a King like Hezekiah. When the temple was restored, "Then the priests arose and blessed the people; and their voices were heard and their prayers came up to God's holy dwelling place, even to heaven" (2 Chr. 30:27). That's some powerful worship.

The picture of Hezekiah is a good one, isn't it? Well, this picture was shattered in 2 Chronicles 32:23-26:

> *Many brought gifts to the Lord in Jerusalem and presents to Hezekiah, King of Judah, so that he was magnified in the sight of all nations from henceforth. Then Hezekiah got sick unto death. He prayed unto the Lord and he spake unto him and He gave him a sign. But, Hezekiah rendered not again according to the benefit done unto him, for his heart was lifted up. Therefore, there was wrath upon him and upon Judah and Jerusalem. Notwithstanding, Hezekiah humbled himself for the pride of his heart, both he and the inhabitants of Jerusalem so that the wrath of the Lord came not upon them in the days of Hezekiah.*

Hezekiah was happy when the people were lifting him

up and exalting him, but he was ungrateful when God healed him. He was actually stealing God's glory and directing the favor of the people to himself. Pride slipped in and before he could get rid of it, it changed him. He tried to make a recovery, but let's look at what his friend Isaiah says about it.

Hezekiah was boastful and gave visiting royalty the grand tour with his pride leading the way. He didn't give God the glory for all that he had, and that's when he got into trouble. Isaiah had the lousy job of telling his friend that the party was over for him. He confronted Hezekiah in the name of the Lord about his pride and told him that everything he had would be lost because of it. He prophesied that Hezekiah's children would become eunuchs and slaves in the palace of their enemy, but because he had repented, all this would happen after he was dead.

Hezekiah's response reveals what was now in his heart: "Good is the word of the Lord which thou hast spoken. He said moreover, For there shall be peace and truth in my days" (Is. 39:8). What about his children, his nation, and his concern for the heart of God? Wouldn't you be overwhelmed by the impending doom of your children and the dreadful fate of a people that you have guided and cared for almost three decades? He knew the mercy of God. Why didn't he beg God to be merciful to those who hadn't committed his crime? No, that part of him was gone. He was self-righteous now.

The man who was famous for his sincerity and passion after the heart of God couldn't find God in anything anymore. He was great, very great, but his greatness opened the door to pride and self-righteousness. The souls of those around Hezekiah were at stake and all he was concerned with was his own comfort and safety in his later years. "Too bad for them. At least I'll have peace until I die."

God's Righteousness

In the same way, the souls of Job's friends were at stake, but he couldn't see it. Job was blinded by his own circumstances and tragedy.

God has created every living thing, and He has given birth to us all. Whether we confess God as our Father, Jesus as our Lord, or the Holy Spirit as our comforter, matters not. God still proclaims, "Come unto Me." God says that He is "not willing that any should perish but that all should come to repentance" (2 Pet. 3:9). The righteousness of God is always seeking souls. What is our righteousness seeking?

If we have our Father's heart, then we should be willing to pray as Jesus prays, and He is praying for our enemies. The Word says that Jesus Christ is the great Mediator between man and God. We should be able to allow Him to shed tears through us. If we shut our eyes and ears to their agony, that's one thing, but to ignore God's agony as His children suffer is a tragedy. Ignoring God's heart causes us to become worse than the enemy that we are so willing to curse. The enemy may not know any better, but we're supposed to have our Father's heart, eyes, and mouth. We're supposed to look like Him, at least a little bit. We need to pray for our enemies as if they are our own children, friends, or relatives perishing, because they are God's. As I said earlier, Paul told Timothy that there are vessels of honor and dishonor in the house of God. Perhaps our enemies have chosen to behave dishonorably. What have we chosen?

Receiving visions from God is not always all it's cracked up to be. I was minding my own business praying one day when the Lord caused me to see a beautiful banquet room with an unbelievable spread of food. I couldn't help but be grateful that I wasn't the one who was going to have to do the dishes afterwards. Gold and crystal were everywhere. The Lord came to me and invited me in, and I knew right away that it was an undeserved privilege. I softly followed the Lord and began to take it all in. The beauty and the glory were awesome! The generosity of the saints one to another and the joy of the angels as souls came to the Kingdom filled the room. The banquet room was a flourishing place!

Then an awful smell began to waft in the air. I asked the Lord what it was and He looked down and to the side but wouldn't answer me. He seemed to be embarrassed or something. I asked the two angels on my left, but they too would not answer and looked away gently. What was this? The smell was killing me. There was a determined looking angel a few feet away, so I asked him what the smell was. He looked me dead square in the face and said, "The smell is you!" What? He continued, "Those who do not have the Father's true heart, the heart that cries for souls, may only be visitors here. The visitors have the smell of the heart of man and not of God. They can never truly take part in this banquet of glory. Your heart has been exposed and now you must leave. Go and find the Father's true heart."

I wept so hard. I had become so busy instructing the saints on purity and fervency that I forgot about those who are slipping off into hell. It's one thing to ignore their screams as they go, but it's somewhat inexcusable when we ignore Christ's screams as they go. They are slipping off completely unnoticed. The Lord cries for them, and we should too.

The Lord stood at the door of this lovely place with a broken heart as He embraced me and sent me on my way. His parting words were, "I look forward to your return when we will have fellowship at this table." He pointed out the spot that had been reserved for me. I long to arrive there again and this time bring souls and not my appetite! Not *my* heart, but *His*. This time as a vessel of honor and not dishonor. If we don't seek God for the lost, who will? If we don't care, maybe no one will! We may be the last "line of defense" for their salvation. We can become so determined to be concerned about our own trouble that we leave no room to be concerned about anyone else's, even God's trouble—the lost going to hell.

I met a woman this year who was not healed when she received prayer. I do not feel that a lack of healing is an exclusive reason or indicator of anything. But, in her case; the spirit revealed that she had so much pride that nothing else could get in—not even her healing. No matter how badly God wanted to give it to her, there was no room inside. She had to give God the "go ahead" for the remodeling of her soul. I sat her down and spent some time with her and let her know very gently that there was gross sin in her life and that was why I couldn't pray for her anymore. I asked her to make it right. I didn't speak of the pride. I wanted her to find it. That was my mistake, as it was never lost!

She stood up, grabbed her coat, and screamed at me in the middle of the congregation and said, "I never sin. I am the most righteous person I know!" Through all of her "righteousness," God couldn't hear her prayers—for her health, for the lost, for nothing. She was crying and screaming for all the wrong reasons.

Travail through us Lord, that your children would be saved.

CHAPTER TEN

Maintaining Your Ways

Though He slay me, yet will I trust in Him; but, I will maintain mine own ways before Him (Job 13:15).

his verse begins nicely with trusting the Lord, but, before the end of it, things take a turn. Job says, "But I will maintain my own ways before the Lord." He is saying, "I will trust you Lord, unto death, but not unto life." Remember, Job wanted to die at this point, so death was a sweet friend to him. He was so bad off that he figured he was going to die anyway. He is saying, "I trust that I will be resurrected in the end. I trust that I will not see hell. I trust that God is the Almighty creator of all things, including me. But, I'm not going to trust Him to pull the fear out of me so that I can live in victory over the things that are making me want to die." Sometimes, we'd rather die than be sanctified. Sometimes, we'd rather die than be purified. Sometimes, we'd rather die than have our ugliness burned out by the One who is a "consuming fire."

Have we arrived at the place where we have faith enough to believe that Jesus Christ died for our sins, but not enough trust to act like it and expect a miracle? It's as if we are

62

saying that we believe in abundant living, but refuse it. What a contradiction!

Job's Stubbornness

So here we have Job. We have established he was a good man, but a man with fear. Now, we find that the fear he had so carefully hidden produced a child called stubbornness. When God tries to pull something rotten out of us, we often resist by bathing it with false humility and the words of righteousness. You can find this trend in Job's statement, "Even if you kill me God, I will still trust you. BUT, as long as I'm alive, I am going to argue with you about my position and attempt to be justified in my opinion. I believe that I am correct in the course that my life has taken. I have a right to it. I believe in God. I have faith for that. But to trust Him to be the kind of God my faith tells me He is? Can't do it!"

Job becomes mad at his friends because they won't let him entertain the grave. Job becomes sarcastic and for several chapters, argues back and forth with his friends, defending his position. Job said, "I'm going to maintain my own ways before the Lord," and he meant it. He maintained his own ways before the Lord and anyone else with guts enough to stand around. As we have seen, his friends eventually became his worst enemies, afflicted with the same spirit that was trying to consume Job.

There was a woman who died on an Easter Sunday at the age of seventy-one. She lived very much alone in West Palm Beach, Florida, and steadfastly maintained her own ways. Upon her death, the Coroner's report read: "Cause of death—malnutrition." After wasting away to 50 pounds, her body gave up. State authorities noted on their investigation papers that her tiny apartment in a run-down neighborhood was an absolute pigpen—the biggest mess you can imagine.

This woman had begged for food from neighbors and picked clothes up for free wherever she could find them. She appeared to be a penniless recluse, a widow who was remembered by no one. Nothing was further from the truth. In the middle of the jungle of her belongings, two keys were found that led officials to safety deposit boxes in two different local banks.

The officials were astounded. They found 700 old AT&T stock certificates, plus hundreds of other valuable certificates, bonds, and solid financial securities, not to mention a pile of cash amounting to over $800,000. The millionaire woman died of starvation while she was maintaining her own ways. The story is that she refused to care for herself and insisted that her children come and do everything for her. If they weren't going to do it, then she would show them that she meant business. I guess they had the same spirit in them, because they evidently showed her that they meant business as well by never seeing her. That's real smart. There is no life in maintaining your own ways.

Elijah's Withdrawal

Elijah is honored above many in the Word of God and with good reason. He was a powerful and dynamic vessel, so highly thought of by the Lord that his "exit plan" from the earth was unlike any other. He left as he lived—in a way that demonstrated the power of God! He is included as one of the three who appeared at the Transfiguration of the Lord Jesus Christ. No doubt, Elijah was a mighty man of God. His type and character is referred to in Revelation, and he holds a special and powerful place in the heart of God. However, he made a mistake that can teach us something. When a powerful person like Elijah makes a mistake, I want to pay attention because it is quite possible that I could fall in the same way (although probably much quicker), given the opportunity and circumstances.

Elijah let his fears get the better of him, as Job did, and it cost him his ministry. In 1 Kings 19, after the miracle at Mt. Carmel, Ahab's wife, Jezebel, sent a messenger to Elijah with the announcement that the next day he would be dead. Elijah immediately lost his courage and ran for his life into the wilderness. Fear will do that to you. In the wilderness, Elijah sat down under a juniper tree and asked God to kill him. An angel appeared and told him to get up, take some nourishment, and go to Horeb, the Mount of God. After traveling for 40 days, Elijah arrived at Mt. Horeb and set up housekeeping in a cave. I don't think that he was sent to Mt. Horeb just so that he could sit in a cave because God appeared to him and demanded, "Elijah, what doest thou here?"

Elijah displayed the same stubbornness as Job did when he proclaimed that he was going to maintain his ways. Elijah said, "I have been very jealous for the Lord God of hosts: because the children of Israel have forsaken thy covenant, thrown down thine altars, and slain thy prophets with the sword; and I, even I only, am left; and they seek my life, to take it away" (1 Ki. 19:14). In other words, Elijah was saying "There are reasons for my behavior. This is the way it is, you can't talk me out of it, God. I've tried to do the right thing. I did all this stuff for you and for your people. Your people have forsaken your word and killed all your prophets. I'm the only one left and now they all want to kill me."

God responded to Elijah, "Get up and go stand upon the mount before me." We now have one of the most terrific visuals of God in the Word. God passed by and a strong wind tore the mountains up and broke all the rocks into pieces.

Then an earthquake shook everything, and fire erupted. And right in the middle of that came a still small voice to further demonstrate God's awesome control and incredible power.

What was Elijah's response? Did he fall on his face before God and worship Him? No, he defensively wrapped his mantle around his face and returned to the cave's entrance. He did not regain his strength and have his calling and purpose rekindled. He was not refreshed and revived with renewed passion after meeting with God Himself. The only place he allowed God's mighty display of power to take him was back to the cave.

God's voice came once again, "What doest thou here?" Elijah's response was less than monumental. He repeated the same excuse as before and didn't allow the revelation to touch him. Unfortunately, the awesome experience on Mt. Horeb wasn't enough to free Elijah from his fears. There was nothing left for God to do because Elijah had set his face and mind toward maintaining his own ways. We will see that Job recovered, but Elijah never did. Although God did not leave him and surely always loved him, the work was taken away from him and Elijah was to anoint Elisha as his successor. The new prophet would have the privilege of carrying twice the power of God that Elijah had.

And God told him in verse 18 that he was not the only prophet left. He had 7,000 other people in Israel who were not Baal worshippers. Maintaining his own ways, cherishing the cave, and choosing death seemed like the only thing for him to do because he had based his decision on fear. Elijah, who was once such a powerful man of God, spent the next 10 years training Elisha to take his place.

Trusting God With Life

Have you trusted God with death and not life? It is certainly easier to die than to live. Trusting God with life means that as Paul said, "To die is gain, to live is Christ." We need to let the Lord introduce us to the powerful concept of who He longs to be in us. Living in Christ means to die to our flesh. What are the issues of the flesh that have grown stronger and louder than Christ in you? Don't waste your time by just reading these words, make them worth something. Make this time, even right now, worth something eternal. Commit to destroying the flesh and all the works of it. Don't "maintain your ways before the Lord" any longer. But instead, trust Him though He slay you. Trust Him though He cause you to live long upon the earth.

May we maintain *His* ways before Him, not ours.

CHAPTER ELEVEN

Judging Ourselves

My foot hath held His steps, His way have I kept and not declined. Neither have I gone back from the commandment of His lips; I have esteemed the words of His mouth more than my necessary food (Job 23:11-12).

Job was developing confidence in his God. More confidence than he ever had before. He always loved the Lord, no doubt. But now his trial was taking him to the next level—the level of faith that holds trust.

If there is no confidence in a relationship, there can be no trust and that relationship will never flourish in the courts of fellowship to enjoy the benefits of trust.

To desire the "words of the Lord more than food," we have to be able to do two things successfully:

1) Judge ourselves and invite God to do the same.

2) Trust God to be merciful and righteous.

Confidence

We should be able to confidently speak God's words as Paul did to the Corinthians in 2 Corinthians 7:1 "Clean up your filthy spirits," and as Peter spoke in 1 Peter 4:17 "For the time has come that judgment must begin at the house of God."

If I'm so busy trying to hide the truth, then my life becomes a lie and the truth is not in me. I can only live in the truth if I can say, "I know whom I have believed." A lack of confidence in the Lord will cause you not to trust Him but to move in fear of what He might or might not do. If you have no confidence in the Lord, then you'll never be able to judge yourself and pray the *Prayer of Job*.

There was a man many years ago who believed that God had called him to make a difference in people's lives, and he committed to that course. He ran for the legislature and was badly beaten. He then decided to open a business. He did so with a partner and the business failed. He spent 17 years of his life paying off the debts of his worthless partner. He continued to have confidence in the fact that he had heard God. Even though everyone seemed to be against him, he persevered because he was confident in what he knew. Confidence builds faith and then produces opportunity for God to prove Himself. Over the course of time, trust emerges.

Next, the man fell in love with a beautiful woman to whom he became engaged, and then she died. He tried to get an appointment with the state government and was denied. He became a candidate for the United States Senate and was badly defeated twice. One failure followed another, with embarrassing rejections and great setbacks. But he continued to move forward in the confidence of his God, trusting that He would be faithful to perform all that He deposited into his heart. That man was Abraham Lincoln, one of the greatest presidents the United States has ever known. Mr. Lincoln had confidence in who God called him to be, and he trusted God to enable him to fulfill that destiny.

Other Biblical Examples

Many other people in the Word of God received their deliverance and saw their "captivity turned" by praying a prayer of mercy and not judgment. After building the temple for God to dwell in, Solomon did not boast to God of his accomplishment. Instead, he humbly declared, "Behold, heaven cannot contain thee; how much less this house which I have built" (2 Chr. 6:18). When Solomon prayed, he asked for the Lord's mercies and forgiveness for himself and his people (2 Chr. 6:25).

Now when Solomon had made an end of praying, the fire came down from heaven and consumed the burnt offering and the sacrifices; and the glory of the Lord filled the house. And the priests could not enter into the house of the Lord because the glory of the Lord had filled the Lord's house (2 Chr. 7:1-2).

God's answer to Solomon's prayer was this:

And the Lord appeared to Solomon by night and said unto him, I have heard thy prayer and have chosen this place to myself for a house of sacrifice. If I shut up heaven that there be no rain, or if I command the locusts to devour the land, or if I send pestilence among my people; If my people, which are called by my name, shall humble themselves, and pray, and seek my face, and turn from their wicked ways, then will I hear from heaven, and will forgive their sin, and will heal their land. Now mine eyes shall be open, and mine ears attent unto the prayer that is made in this place (2 Chr. 7:12-15).

God always responds to the humble prayers of His people.

Hannah, the mother of Samuel, is another example of someone who put her confidence in God. "Hannah was in bitterness of soul and prayed unto the Lord and wept sore" (1 Sam. 1:10). Part of her bitterness was because of her husband's other wife always making fun of her barrenness. She prayed, begging God to judge her, not to punish the other woman. She prayed out of a pure heart and was not mad at God because she couldn't have children. She wanted a child, but was willing to hear God first.

She trusted God to judge her correctly. She trusted the Lord enough to judge her, forgive her, and walk in the power of that judgment. She became vulnerable to the Spirit of the Lord so that He was able to bless and empower her.

Let's look at Jonah and his prayer. Jonah was mad at God and a lot of people. When we forget who God is and lose that revelation, we can become "disconnected" from Him and be provoked to react incorrectly because of the things around us.

Then "Jonah prayed unto the Lord his God out of the fish's belly." When he prayed from the belly of the fish, God turned his captivity. The meaning here is that he judged himself and invited God to do the same. Later in scripture it is said that Jonah "remembered the Lord" (Jonah 2:1). We must remember who He is and who we are not, and always keep in mind the power and mercy of God.

God had mercy on the Ninevites when they judged themselves as being in error and moved in true repentance and humility. Jonah didn't like God's mercy toward the Ninevites because it made him look bad and his prophetic utterance to appear wrong. But, our God is a God of mercy first, if we will truly repent. Jonah quickly lost the revelation of who God is that he earlier paid such a high price to get.

It's very hard to repent or to humble ourselves if we haven't enlisted Job's prayer first and judged ourselves. One allows the other to come. Without the *Prayer of Job* active in our lives, true humility and repentance are usually a destination we strive for and rarely a place where we arrive.

CHAPTER TWELVE

From Hearing to Seeing

I have heard of thee by the hearing of the ear: but now mine eye seeth thee. Wherefore, I abhor myself and repent in dust and ashes (Job 42:5-6).

Unlike Elijah, who stubbornly maintained his own ways and plans even after God demonstrated His power, when Job finally saw God, it changed him completely. As a result, Job saw himself as God saw him and repented in the dust, putting ashes upon himself. Instead of judging his friends, he judged himself. We can't pray the *Prayer of Job* unless we abhor our own selfish motives and repent of them.

In the midst of difficult trials, we must keep our heart and mind on where the Lord is taking us. In order to move from a relationship that *hears* about God to a fellowship that *sees* Him face to face, Job would have to see his need for it and crave it more than his own life. In the end, he would have to abandon his own needs and fears to obtain it.

Political cartoonist Sydney Harris once said, "Since most of us would rather be admired for what we do, rather than for who we are, we are normally willing to sacrifice character for conduct and integrity for achievement." How true, hence the trouble with our "vision." Hearing is much easier. When we really begin to *see* who Christ is, everything else pales in comparison. Clear vision causes us to see ourselves clearly as God does and to desire to move in integrity. Clear vision requires honesty. Before we truly see God, we must first see ourselves.

God was not willing to leave Job in his emotional misery, so He appeared in a whirlwind and asked him why he listened to people without knowledge. God reminded him that He is in charge of everything and told him to get up and act like a man and answer His questions:

Did you give the peacock her wings, did you give the ostrich her feathers? Do the eagles mount up at your command? Does the hawk fly because of your wisdom? Did you make the horse strong? Where were you when I formed the foundations of the earth? Did I take counsel of you when I formed the earth? When the morning stars sang together and all the sons of God shouted for joy, where were you? Have you commanded the morning to come forth since the beginning of your days? Have you walked in the bottom of the sea and have the gates of death been opened up unto thee? Where does the light dwell? Where is the place of darkness? There is no man who can cause it to rain! Do you know the ordinances of heaven and can you set the dominion of it in the earth? Can you lift up your voice into the clouds and cause the abundance of waters to cover you. Does the lightning come and speak unto you and shout, "Here we are"? Do you hunt the prey for the lion and provide food for the raven when their young are hungry? Do you have an arm like God

*and can your voice thunder like His? Who are you
to instruct me?* (Job 38-41)

At this point, Job's fear of life was torn out and laid to
rest, and his trust in God emerged. Job remembered the
greatness of His God as he stood in awe of Him. He came to
his senses in Chapter 40 and responded, "I will lay my hand
upon my mouth, once I have spoken; but I will not answer
twice, I will proceed no further." Smart man! He is saying,
"I'm not saying nothin'." The intent of his heart became
"I'm done! Whatever You want, God, whatever You say,
wherever You're going, that's where I'm going." His revelation of who God is has been restored.

The woman with the "issue of blood," the one who
"touched the hem of Christ's garment" knew what it was
like to go from hearing to seeing. She was broke, rejected,
humiliated, sick, and looked pretty hopeless and alone. She
had been ill for 12 years and probably heard the words,
"Unclean, defiled, unworthy" shouted at her often. Pretty
depressing.

The only way one could touch the hem of someone's garment would be to crawl down on the ground. Maybe she was
too weak to walk or was trying to avoid the people. The
Bible says that when she touched the hem of His garment,
she was immediately healed. Jesus recognized it at once, as
it says in Luke 8:46, "Somebody hath touched me: for I per-
ceive that virtue is gone out of me." What made her different than the multitude?

The disciples asked Jesus, "Master, the multitude throng
thee and press thee, why sayest thou, 'Who touched me?'"
Trembling, the woman went forward and confessed. She announced her condition before everyone and declared that
she was healed, giving glory to God. I'm happy for her, but

what about that touch? The Lord didn't say, "Who is pressing and thronging me?" There was a difference between the woman and the rest of the people—the crowd that was pressing and thronging Him.

To press Him meant that they were trying to put their will upon Christ, approaching Him to insist on having their own ways. They were saying, "Lord, we don't really want to see You, to know You, to walk in fellowship with You. We just want to have a relationship where we can come and get what we want when we want it, but if the going gets too tough, well, then we're outta here." It went beyond insisting on their way, it moved into preventing and forbidding His. They could only hear themselves and not see Him. When all you have done is heard of Him, your affection for Him will never be greater than the affection you have for yourself. So, when they were later offered favors to shout, "Crucify Him," they didn't hesitate to do it. But once you've really *seen* the Lord, you only desire to shout "crucify" to your own flesh. You no longer hide from the cost of revival, but instead pursue the cost, more than the revival itself.

The woman who was healed simply "touched" His garment. *Webster's* definition of touch reads, "to handle or feel gently usually with the intent to understand or appreciate." *Strong's* explains the intent of her heart further by a literal translation which means "to attach yourself to and be set on fire." Her heart was seeking who Jesus was. Yes, she desired what He could do, but more than anything, she believed what she had heard about Him and came to see Him more clearly. She was willing to lose who she was to gain who He is. It was only then that she could be caught on fire and changed.

To touch Christ, we need to be in agreement with Him or the connection won't work. The fabric will continually slip away from us. The people that *press*, give God an instruction book on their relationship. The ones that *touch*, are after the understanding of His truth, and they have the courage not to fear what it does to them. They expect to come out with nothing but the ability to see Him because they crave fellowship. He meets their expectation with more mercy than they figured on and more love than they can hold. How the Lord adores those who reach out and touch Him! Will we be among the ones who "touch" Jesus or the multitude who "press" Him?

All the turmoil in any trial is not bigger than God. Watch Him turn it into a powerful future!

CHAPTER THIRTEEN

Job's Prayer

And the Lord turned the captivity of Job, when he prayed for his friends [who by now were basically, his enemies]; *also, the Lord gave Job twice as much as he had before* (Job 42:10).

J ob trusted God enough to pray for his enemies. In an earlier example, we saw that Ellie had to trust God to cause her son's death to be worth something as she embraced prayer, deep intercession, and travail for his murderer.

When Job prayed for his "friends," it had to be tough. He had lost everything, even his precious children. All he had left was a nagging wife and boils on his body "from the sole of his feet to the top of his head." I'll admit, life was miserable for Job, but every action has a reaction and every situation has a consequence.

Before Job prayed for them, God spoke to Job's friends, "My servant Job will pray for you, and I will accept his prayer and not deal with you according to your folly" (Job 42:8). This was a test for Job as much as for his friends. When he prayed for his enemies, Job had to trust the Lord as never before. He had to quit fighting his trouble and find God in it.

Praying for our enemies is risky business because they will receive our blessings and our favor along with our forgiveness. Job came to the place where he could give his friends all of those things. He gave them the kind of blessings that beg God to "go easy" on them and bless them, birthed out of his desire to know the heart of God.

When Job prayed for his friends, he judged himself in the process. Thereupon God not only released him from his captivity, but He opened Job's eyes to see Him more clearly. When he successfully came out the other side of this trial, he counted it a privilege to pray for them. To pray this prayer from the deepest spot in the heart, we have to completely trust God. To fully forgive and at the same time judge ourselves in error, we have to trust God more than we have ever done before. It's a leap from a tall building without a cape!

Relationship or Fellowship?

When we pray for our enemies, we have to trust that the Lord is going to take care of us. This is when we find out what kind of communion we have with our God. Is it relationship or fellowship?

Faith rests in relationship. Trust rests in fellowship. I have a relationship with my children. I am their mother. That's our relationship, and it will always be true. If I gave birth and never spoke to them again, I would still be their biological mother. But, if I desire fellowship with my children, I need to show up at their ball games, make their favorite meals, spend time with them, and create memories. That's fellowship. There is an immense difference.

The *Prayer of Job* cannot be prayed from a position of relationship. We'll never let it happen. But fellowship will embrace it. Fellowship will take what we have and give it to others. It lives to give and survives by doing it. Relationship doesn't mind taking and consuming. Many times relationship "figures it's got it coming!"

If we're going to pray the *Prayer of Job*, we have to be able to judge ourselves honestly. We must be willing to hear what God says is wrong with us and go beyond what we figure is wrong. If we are very still, we can discover such truths.

If we looked at what was inside of us a little more, we wouldn't have so much time to snoop in other people's business. At a church in California, a woman came in toward the end of service during prayer. It didn't take a genius to figure out her profession. During prayer, the Lord delivered her from drug addiction and prostitution. She came running to Jesus like a kid through a sprinkler on a hot day. Her joy clearly radiated from the depths of her being. She said that she almost didn't come by, but was so glad that she did. When asked why she almost didn't come, her response broke my heart and I had her repeat it to the pastor. "I wasn't going to come because I was afraid of being judged." Is that the reputation of who the Church has become? A house of judgment toward the lost and dying? *We must honestly judge ourselves first, and if we do, our judgment of others will turn into compassion for them.*

If the Church is the hospital of the Lord (since He said He came for the sick) then shouldn't the lost and hurting run to our house for refuge and help? They run to the emergency room when they break their arms, so why won't they come to us when they break their hearts? It's because we haven't prepared the way for it, and they know it! There is too much of us in the flag that is waving above our sanctuaries. The lost and sick are looking for help, not more problems.

I need to pray the *Prayer of Job* because I'm desperate to be refined and perfected, not because I'm desperate to be delivered or blessed. If I have Christ in me, then I shouldn't be hungry and thirsty anymore. But we always tend to want more, more, more. What about getting full, staying full, living full, and giving to others from the abundance of that fullness? When we pray out of abundance, it is entirely different than when we pray out of lack. We often grab the wrong thing that just covers up our problem and then move on. As a result, we will quickly require another spiritual or emotional "fix," but refuse to be honest about the root of our troubles. We concentrate on beholding the small fruit that we have, so the ugly root of our weeds will never be exposed. We often dance and rejoice over the fruit, not realizing it is small, spoiled, distasteful, and questionably "out of season."

Abundance

Anyone who goes through the elements that lead up to praying the *Prayer of Job* will find themselves in a position to receive abundance. When we are operating out of this spirit that wants truth at all costs, the true spirit of abundance, then we are not afraid to pray abundance on others. We will search our own hearts for ways to give more, causing us to lean on Christ for our strength.

When the rich young ruler asked the Lord, "What do I need to do to inherit eternal life," the Lord told him to follow the commandments. The man replied that he'd been doing that since he was a child, and the Lord said to him in Luke 18:22 "....Yet lackest thou one thing, sell all that thou hast, and distribute unto the poor, and thou shalt have treasure in heaven and come, follow me." When the man heard it, he was very sad the Bible says, because "he was very rich."

You see, this man was bound by the law and not by love. He had a relationship with God, not fellowship. He was not willing to judge himself. He didn't trust the Lord to give him back his wealth or to take his need or desire for it away. He was very sorry and very rich, but he *could have been* a fired-up disciple. He couldn't follow Jesus as a disciple because he refused to judge what was in his heart. This kept him from taking advantage of the best thing that was ever going to happen to him. He refused to find out what was on the other side of radical obedience.

Yes, this man's inability to pray the *Prayer of Job* cost him more than it should have. If he would have judged what was in his heart, the Holy Spirit would have revealed the truth to him so that he could be released to live in freedom and liberty. He was so worried about what he would lose that he never got around to pondering what he would gain.

Twice as Much

The Word says that the Lord blessed Job more than at the beginning. He had seven more sons and three more daughters "and in all the land were no women found so fair as the daughters of Job." He lived for four generations afterwards.

Job had the privilege of gaining everything twice—livestock, opportunity, friends, money, and children who loved one another. What a blessing that is. When his second family came, each child was probably filled with "joy unspeakable and full of glory." The joy, love, and abundance they walked around in had to have been beyond what man had ever known or seen. Job was blessed with the thrill of watching God bring him not only everything twice, but he was able to see the miracle of "twice as good" the second time around.

CHAPTER FOURTEEN

Find a Mirror, Not a Telescope!

Jesus declares "Judge not, that ye be not judged.
For with what judgment you judge; you shall be
judged: and with what measure ye mete, it shall be
measured to you again. And why beholdest thou the
mote that is in thy brother's eye, but considerest not
the beam that is in thine own eye? Or how wilt thou
say to thy brother, Let me pull out the mote out of
thine eye; and, behold, a beam is in thine own eye?
Thou hypocrite, first cast out the beam out of thine
own eye: and then shalt thou see clearly to cast out
the mote out of thy brother's eye" (Matt. 7:1-5).

The meaning of the word "judge" in these verses is to "decide or distinguish mentally or judicially, to call into question." We need to practice doing that to ourselves, not others. "For with what judgment you judge, you shall be judged," means that when we judge another, we are also setting forth the means by which we desire to (and shall be) judged by God. Instead, let us have God's compassionate heart toward others and He will see to it that we reap the benefits. We can trust Him. The Lord longs to bless us, but we are so busy judging others that we can't catch those blessings, no matter how abundant they may be. Often, no matter how desperate He is to give them to us, He must wait upon us to change.

Sometimes the prophetic utterance hangs on the hinge of our obedience when God says, "if you will, then I will...." Of course, we often forget about our end of the deal and then put the blame on God and call Him unfaithful. God wants us to rid our souls of the jealousy, insecurity, doubt, and rage that consume us. God brings a prophetic word to motivate us to make more room for Him in order to see the fulfillment of it. However, too often we just sit back and ponder the word instead of pursuing it. The thief comes to steal, but we must not allow him to be successful against God's desire and intention for us.

Righteous Judgment

There is a thing called "righteous judgment." The Lord said in John 7:24 to "Judge not according to the appearance, but judge righteous judgment." Righteous judgment is one of the occupations of the Holy Spirit, not the human spirit. In this verse, we're told to "get into the spirit of God" and allow Him to be the judge.

Righteous judgment is made by God alone and is a righteous determination of our heart's intent. The "judging" that we are to do is the judging of the "fruit" as we are told in the Word, by observing and discerning our motives and outcomes. The "righteous judgment" by God and the "fruit judgment" by His people are vastly different.

One evening when the room was full and the meeting was running very late, there was a multitude of people who still needed prayer. There were several people gathered around a man in a wheelchair, all excited about what God would do. Although most of them were from the church,

84

they didn't know this man. I didn't know him either; but it seemed to me, the miracle that he needed was to accept Christ as his Savior.

So, I asked him if he wanted to let the Lord take control of his life and he said, "No. I came here to get healed. I believe in God. My Mom taught me years ago. I'm just not ready to live for Him right now. But, in spite of me, He is still God and I'm still His child. I'm not a very good kid, kind of rebellious and all, but that doesn't change the fact that He is God. The word around town is that people are in here getting miracles, so I came for mine."

"Just like that?"

"Yes Ma'am." Well, that's good enough for me. We prayed and that man got up out of his wheelchair and walked out. I still pray for his salvation, hoping he will find the way soon.

The point of this story is this: All the people standing around him became infuriated when he was healed. They couldn't stand it. I started laughing because it was so bizarre to see these "Christians" flipping out because someone got a blessing that either 1) they had not deemed him worthy to receive or 2) they wanted for themselves! They began telling me that it couldn't be God that healed him, and I laughed even harder.

I told them, "The fruit is this: the guy is walking! It was either the devil or the Lord who did it. Pick one. If it's the devil, you need to repent for being deceived and throw me out. If it's the Lord, you need to get out of the way and let God have His way."

They were angry because the miracle was forcing them judge themselves, and they didn't like it. Judging ourselves is the best gift, and we should learn to love it. If we are busy with the mirror, we won't have time for the telescope!

Judging someone else brings radical, ungodly behavior

into our spirits. Just 10 minutes earlier, they were sur-
rounding this man, slobbering all over him and telling him,
"The Lord loves you, brother." How could he believe that?
By their behavior, I would have thought the man made the
right choice by "getting out of Dodge" as soon as he could.
The condition of their hearts was exposed by the judgment
coming from their mouth. Some repented in horror, unable
to believe that such ugliness was dwelling in them. Others
continued on a self-righteous tirade with theology and doc-
trine, bound to defend their position. The Lord very quickly
caused them to know that this was His business, not theirs.
His righteousness, not theirs. The man had faith and God
chose to honor it. Who are we to judge? We are not to be in-
spectors of someone else's heart, but farmers that tend the
soil of our own.

Knowing God

Daniel understood the prayer of travail and bending before God because Daniel understood who God is. We cannot
ask for the mercy of God if we are bathed in our own righteousness. We must gain His mercy to pray the *Prayer of
Job,* the prayer that set Job free and that can set us free.
The *Prayer of Job* turned his captivity and is ready to turn
ours, for the glory of God.

> *O my God, incline thine ear, and hear; open thine
> eyes and behold our desolations, and the city which
> is called by thy name: for we do not present our
> supplications before thee for our righteousness, but
> for thy great mercies* (Daniel 9:18).

Daniel was a boy, probably somewhere between the ages
of 12 and 16, when he was taken into a foreign country and

treated barely better than a slave. This all changed later because Daniel carried the favor of God with him. The kings put gold on him and caused him to be a great governor in Babylon. But when they commanded him to quit praying, he wouldn't do it. When they said to eat their pagan idol food, he wouldn't do it. He refused to defile his body or his spirit, because he wouldn't disobey his God. Even when he was thrown in with lions, he didn't quiver or shake. Daniel had confidence in his God; he knew Him to be righteous and merciful. Confidence comes from being able to share opportunities with the Lord, living our faith, and developing trust in Him. Daniel knew that God could be trusted, but many of us aren't too sure about that.

Proper Judgment

Proper judgment does not mean we are to condemn ourselves or anyone else. Under the inspiration of the Holy Spirit, proper judgment uses discernment to discover error within ourselves. In other words, we use a mirror to examine our own hearts and not a telescope to examine someone else's. When we seek forgiveness from the Lord, the Holy Spirit allows us to move on quickly and not live in the bondages of the past. There is no condemnation in Christ, only freedom and liberty.

When I judge you, I'm chasing down your error and missing mine. As a result, I will more than likely condemn you. Jesus said, "If I be lifted up, I will draw all men unto me." The Lord will show others what's wrong with their darkness through our light if we would simply turn on our light and stop shouting at their darkness. As Matthew 5:16 says, "Let your light shine before men, that they may see your good deeds and praise your Father in heaven."

The light is in you. Just let it burn and shine. Live a life in God bright enough for others to see your light. Advertise your light; don't judge their darkness. The righteousness of Christ will be revealed through living a Christ-like life, not through condemning those who don't.

There were a group of people who got involved in a cult of satanic worship. Years went by, and they were growing in what they considered strength and power. Then one day, they came by and wanted to see who had the greater power. Well, you and I know that Christ does. The Holy Spirit made a very short event of what they counted on lasting for days. They were quickly delivered from demonic possession and set free from pain and horror. The redemption of the lost and hurting is always a beautiful thing to watch.

During this time of deliverance, a vision occurred that everyone could see. It paralyzed many for quite awhile and sent others into uncontrollable weeping. The vision showed God sitting on a throne, very much high and lifted up, in what appeared to be a courtroom setting. I was just outside the courtroom, with the scene in plain view. The others watched from my living room in an agony of fear. In front of this throne was furniture as one might see in a courtroom, with Jesus at one table and Satan at the other. Satan began to spew venomous remarks about the people in my living room, urging God to have nothing to do with them for they had killed their own children as sacrifices unto Satan and defiled God in the worst of ways. They had hurt the children of God with unspeakable acts and caused abomination to enter into the church. Satan proclaimed over and over again that he had a claim to them because they had pledged allegiance to him.

Jesus walked back and forth in front of the throne and kept making the same statement over and over again, never flinching or wavering, "But, Father, I died for them. I died for them." This went on and on. The calm, steady power in His voice could shake the universe, and it probably did.

God heard both sides and gazed at Jesus with a look of adoration that would refuse Him nothing. God stood and said, "The defense is enough; Satan, loose them; they are set free in the name of my Son. The blood is sufficient!" Jesus kept using the same line of defense over and over again, and it was more than enough because of the price that was paid. The name of Jesus will always be enough. May we attempt to be worthy of that death and walk in His resurrection.

The righteousness of Jesus Christ was revealed to that group and changed them forever. Only One is righteous!

There is one lawgiver, who is able to save and to destroy: who art thou that judgest another? (James 4:12)

CHAPTER FIFTEEN

Did They Put You in Bondage When You Weren't Looking?

Jesus said, "Therefore, if you bring your gift to the altar and there remember that your brother has something against you, leave your gift there before the altar and go your way. First be reconciled to your brother and then come and offer your gift" (Matt. 5:23-24).

To reconcile is to change thoroughly. The only way to resolve a conflict that we didn't start is to lay the problem down and try to reconcile hearts, not issues. Agree to disagree. Come into agreement with your brother on what you can agree on, not every aspect and avenue of the opinions that you don't.

When Job's friends turned into his enemies and were giving him fits, God let them know He was not pleased. Then God told Job that His wrath was kindled against the three friends and insisted that they go back over to Job's place and have a prayer meeting. He wanted them to be reconciled with Job, not have a discussion about who was right and who was wrong. And in this prayer meeting, He didn't want the friends saying anything. I guess they've said enough. He tells them in Job 42:8 "my servant Job shall

90

pray for you: for him will I accept; lest I deal with you after your folly." God was saying that He was not ready to hear them quite yet, but He would hear Job's prayer for them. How many times is God waiting for us to pray for someone and we just won't do it? This was the point of true recovery in Job's captivity. When he prayed for his friends, God set him free from his troubles.

If his heart wasn't right, if he hadn't gone through all his trials, he may never have been able to give wings to this prayer.

Reconciliation

The book of Philemon is a perfect example of reconciliation. In fact, it is so perfect, its truths are universal. I used it as a main text in California State Universities and businesses for years when I taught business management, ethics, team building, and conflict resolution.

This is Paul's intervention into a domestic secular situation bringing salvation, reconciliation, and forgiveness. Onesimus was a slave, and Philemon was his master. Onesimus ran away, crashed into Paul, and found Christ! He became a big help to Paul, who at the time of this writing was enjoying his first prison term in Rome. Paul made it clear that a reconciliation between Philemon and Onesimus needed to take place.

Philemon was a wealthy man who lived in Colosse and had a church in his home. His son was a minister, and he and his wife were also involved in the work. Paul encouraged Philemon not to think of Onesimus any longer as a slave, but as a brother in the Lord. He spent time describing the new relationship they could enjoy if Philemon would just allow it.

When Onesimus showed up, he was received as a

brother in the Lord. Paul saw to it that they laid down their past and looked toward the future they could have in the Lord. To be reconciled, remember, is to be thoroughly changed. Reconciliation doesn't take prisoners; it just gets the job done.

But when we have done nothing wrong and are being unfairly attacked, it is difficult to deal with. One time a woman came into my life who was horribly rude, not to anyone else, but regularly to me. I finally asked the Lord what I was doing wrong and He showed me Matthew 5:23-24:

Therefore, if you are offering your gift at the altar and there remember that your brother has something against you, leave your gift there in front of the altar. First go and be reconciled to your brother; then come and offer your gift.

In other words, God said that we must be reconciled with others before we can come back to the altar of God and enjoy Jesus. I didn't like these verses. I tried to get out of them because I had asked her before if I had done anything to offend or upset her and she kept saying, "No, not at all." But you and I both know that what she really meant was "Yes, but I'm not telling." So, I was pretty much being held hostage by her emotions. I don't make a good hostage, but I was stuck. I couldn't go forward in my Christian walk. I asked the Lord, "Let me get this straight. I'm not welcome at Your altar until I reconcile with this person who doesn't want to be reconciled?" "That's right," He replied. "Okay."

Basically, it really wasn't about her willingness to reconcile. It was about the fact that she had a problem, and I didn't do anything to solve it or make a fair effort to care. Once we make the "beyond what's reasonable" effort, we cannot *make* them respond, only pray they will and make ourselves available when they do. After that, we are not bound to their anger or attitude any longer. The Lord is looking for our willingness to submit to His authority in all things.

I found a day when I loved the Lord more than my pride and went to her house. Once inside, I locked the door behind me and said, "I don't make a good hostage, and you're not going to keep me in bondage. You have to be reconciled to me according to Matthew 5 so that I can move on. I won't allow you to do this to me. So, you're going to tell me why you hate me so much, and we are going to put an end to this right now!"

She replied that she had an appointment, so I told her to cancel it. I wouldn't let her leave. I told her that *she* was going to be a hostage now, until she confessed what was the trouble between us. What choice did she have? She eventually confessed jealousy and resentment toward me. She said that I hadn't done anything. It was her problem, and she would deal with it alone.

I said, "No way! This ugliness has flopped on my life now, and the Lord has required me to come over here and help you, in order to help myself!" She cried and cried, asked for forgiveness and cried some more. I apologized for not being more sensitive to her needs and began to edify her in her giftedness. We both cried and visited most of the day. We joined together for a powerful time of prayer and told the devil that he had lost. He can never win against honesty and obedience to the Word. We ate lunch and had some chocolate—the stuff of friendship! We have been very good friends ever since. In fact, now instead of spreading lies about me birthed out of her own pain and wounds, she has become my great defender and a minister of healing to many.

There are those people who refuse to be reconciled. They belong to God once we have sincerely made our efforts. But, we must sincerely make the effort first. Then leave it alone. As the saying goes, "You can take a horse to water, but you can't make 'em drink." Bring the water and pet the horse gently. Do the very best that you can. Then, leave it with Him.

CHAPTER SIXTEEN

Enemy Praying

Ye have heard that it hath been said, Thou shalt love thy neighbor and hate thine enemy. But I say unto you, Love your enemies, bless them that curse you, do good to them that hate you, and pray for them which despitefully use you, and persecute you. That ye may be the children of your Father which is in heaven for He maketh His sun to rise on the evil and on the good and sendeth rain on the just and on the unjust. For if ye love them which love you, what reward have ye? Do not even the publicans the same? And if ye salute your brethren only, what do ye more than others? Do not even the publicans so? Be ye therefore perfect even as your Father which is in heaven is perfect (Matthew 5:43-48).

Prayer will either exhaust you or empower you, depending on whose strength you are using when you do it—yours or the Holy Spirit's. Yes, prayer is laborious. We are tired afterward, but we are refreshed. We are ruined, but we are renewed. We travail, but we are triumphant.

Jesus says to bless and pray for those who despitefully use and persecute us. Scripture tells us that if we will do this, then we can be called "children of God." So, it's reasonable to say that if we don't pray for our enemies and attempt to bless them, we cannot be true children of God. We could probably be acquaintances, but not children of God and joint heirs with Jesus. The Lord is saying to enlist the prayer called "Enemy Praying."

Enemy praying is about three things:

1) Praying for my enemies
2) Worshiping God because of my enemies
3) Blessing my enemies.

Jesus knew that we would have need to pray the *Prayer of Job*. That's why He said to forgive "seventy times seven each day." He knew that we would need help praying it, that's why He spoke these words as recorded by Matthew.

> *But I say unto you, Love your enemies, bless them that curse you, do good to them that hate you, and pray for them which despitefully use you, and persecute you* (Matt. 5:44).

1. **Pray for them**.

Okay, now the rub really starts. The word "Pray" here means to "earnestly supplicate (humbly seek God) with strength, seeking direction."

I can't earnestly supplicate for you if the best I can do is worry about me and hate you. I can't seek direction for you if I'm in the way. And I can't seek the direction of God, concerning me, if I refuse humility and the strength of God to do so. It takes strength to find out the truth. It's a scary prospect, but the Word does say that we can "do all things through Christ who strengthens us." Be willing and let Him.

Maybe it's not all the other guy's fault, maybe you can learn something along this road too.

God brings those difficult people across our paths, so that we will pray for them. God is trusting us with a very hard task and heavy responsibility: to pray for our enemies. There may be no other way to reach them. Most of the time, all we do is beg to be delivered from them! Often we think they deserve to go to hell, half the time, we wish they would!

> *But I say unto you, Love your enemies, bless them that curse you, do good to them that hate you, and pray for them which despitefully use you, and persecute you* (Matt. 5:44).

2. **Worship God.**

The translation of a portion of these words is: "To worship God because of them and to pray your own blessings upon them." It's one thing to pray for them, but to give up my stuff for them?

Worshiping the Lord because of them means we have to be thankful for the trial, and trust God for the outcome. To do this we'd have to "Be anxious for nothing." and "In everything give thanks, for this is the Will of God in Christ Jesus concerning you." To do this, we have to be more concerned about the Lord's perfect work in us than our own work in us or His perfect work in someone else.

When we praise God, He comes to where we are. When we worship God, we go to where He is. To truly worship, we must be on God's agenda, not our own. We must allow Him to introduce us to His thoughts and plans.

Pray until you can speak blessings upon them—not generic, hypocritical blessings, but instead, pray the kind that come from the heart, that you are not in control of, but the Holy Spirit is. Pray as if someone you love will be destroyed if you don't. Pray the prayer that causes you to worship the Lord in spirit and in truth.

> *But I say unto you, Love your enemies, bless them that curse you, do good to them that hate you, and pray for them which despitefully use you, and persecute you* (Matt. 5:44).

3. Bless them.

A further translation of "bless" here means "to praise and speak prosperity into. Religiously speak blessings into someone. Thinking and speaking well of."

When's the last time you went bragging about the great qualities of your enemy? Doing that will help you worship God because of them instead of complaining to God about them. When's the last time you tried to understand the ailment of your tormentor? Often, we aren't very good at that. We are good at reminding God that His Word says, vengeance is His, and He will repay. We want Him to get busy repaying them for all the evil they are doing to us, His good kids.

We may curse our enemies' plans for us and take away the power their words have over us; but as for our enemies themselves, we must leave them to God. They're His trouble, not ours.

A church in the Midwest was interviewing for pastors and two men preached on the same text, "Evildoers will go to hell." When the vote came down between those two men, the decision makers voted in the second man. When explaining the reason for voting the way they did, since the men used the same text, they gave this reply, "When the second man emphasized that the lost will be going to hell, he said it with tears in his eyes and with concern in his voice. The first preacher almost seemed to enjoy the thought and gloat over it."

Can we pray for others while there is still time? I know that we are sick of our tormentors and it seems that our persecutors are getting all the great things that we should be getting, some even at our expense; but until that's okay with us, we'll stay in bondage over it.

CHAPTER SEVENTEEN

Your Captivity Will Turn

So the Lord blessed the latter end of Job, more than his beginning...After this Job lived 140 years and saw his sons and his sons' sons, even to the fourth generation. So when Job died, he was old and full of days (Job 42:12,16-17).

Allow your captivity to turn. It's God's will and desire for you to live full of days! We are supposed to go from "glory to glory" on this earth in spirit and flesh. It should get better and better. If it's not, maybe there is a bondage in your heart. Have you found it? Can you pray the *Prayer of Job* yet? Or have "they" not earned or deserved your prayers yet? Sometimes your freedom depends upon their blessing!

Here's the Lord's desire and will for you:

For I know the thoughts that I think toward you, saith the Lord, thoughts of peace, and not of evil, to give you an expected end. Then shall ye call upon me, and ye shall go and pray unto me and I will hearken unto you and ye shall seek me and find me when ye shall search for me with all your heart. I

*will be found of you saith the Lord: and I will turn
away your captivity and I will gather you from all
the nations, and from all the places whither I have
driven you, saith the Lord; and I will bring you
again to the place from whence you were carried
away captive* (Jer. 29:11-14).

Power of His Promises

For the above blessings to come to pass in our lives, we
must pray the prayer of honesty and reckless abandon toward the Lord's desires. We need to pray the *Prayer of Job*
so that the power of these promises can be bestowed upon
us and our children and their children. It's big enough to
slop onto our neighbor's children too. God is still waiting; He
always is.

There was a legal issue I was involved with that had
been going on for over four years. I became implicated in
corporate issues that were not my affair. Nevertheless, there
I was in the middle of a nightmare that would not go away.
Angry, aggressive people wanted one thing and one thing
only—for someone to pay. They couldn't get to anyone else,
so they chose me. Maybe you've been there. I prayed for deliverance. I prayed for justice. I prayed for the will of God.
Then I prayed for deliverance again.

One morning when I was praying, the Lord began to
show me that these parties involved were on their way to
hell. He gave me a revelation of how He feels when people
suffer in hell. He caused me to feel a portion of His horrible
pain and anguish. He caused me to know what it would feel
like if my children weren't secure in His arms. He let me feel
His added anguish when His children who call Him Father
won't pray for the others who don't know the way or who
have lost their way to Him. His heart breaks for the lost.
Why do we deafen our ears to His cries over their suffering?

The agony of this revelation was so horrible that for days I could hardly function. I had to keep running off to be alone, screaming and crying under the burden of what I was seeing. I saw the horror of people with no peace and no Jesus, a future without hope. It's too much to bear. It's as if it were my own children suffering in eternal flames. I screamed and howled, begging God for their souls. *Surely I shall never shower, eat or sleep again*, I thought. We must understand that the Lord loves our adversaries, the ones who are persecuting and despitefully using us. Let us feel His pain and be provoked to pray like we never have before. Scripture says "to love the Lord with all thine heart, mind and soul and to love thy neighbor as thyself." Trouble is, I don't even *like* them, how can I *love* them? Without loving them through Jesus, I don't suppose I can. Flesh is like that.

After 10 days of gut-wrenching horror and screaming unto God for their souls, the Lord impressed me to turn to the book of Job. He said to my heart, "I will now turn your captivity as I did Job's because you have prayed the prayer that I will hear." This book has emerged from that moment.

Strange thing, I no longer prayed about the court case or worried about it. All I could do was cry for Jesus, who was losing those He loves to eternal flames, and weep for those who would suffer those flames.

The next day, out of nowhere, completely unsolicited, the attorney called to announce they were going to dismiss several of the cases. As far as I was concerned, it was a miracle right up there with the parting of the Red Sea.

Yes, praying for your enemies is risky business. They will receive your blessings, favor, and forgiveness! They might end up like the Ninevites and make you look bad and call it godly. Job's prayer? He judged himself wrong and prayed life into his enemies. Are we willing to pray like that? Our Lord is weeping over them. How can we just walk by? God is trusting us to pray for our enemies, and we need to trust Him to take care of us as we attempt to bless them. Job made his year of torment count as he ever so carefully prayed for his friends, seeking God's desires and not his own.

One day, a woman came for prayer, and God wasn't moving upon her. Sometimes when that happens, it's just not time. It's better to inquire of God about His timing for these things and avoid confusion and disappointment later. But, we don't always get to that place when we are in pain. It's somehow easier—more complicated, but easier—to just ask God to heal us. Anyway, this woman came for prayer and the healing wouldn't come, but it really felt like it should have. So, we talked. She was the sweetest little lady. I told her that I wasn't sure what was up, but that I did feel it was her time to be healed. I told her that maybe she should have someone else pray for her.

She wasn't hearing that, so we prayed again. This time we were not seeking healing but seeking truth. The Lord revealed that she had a root of bitterness against her mother. She was able to trace that thing back 22 years, to the beginning of her back pain, subsequent arthritis, and now cancer. She loved her mother dearly and couldn't remember thinking a bad thought about her. But, there it was, hiding in her soul, tearing up the lawn of her spirit. *She never inquired of God as deeply as she did that day, so she never saw the truth.* It was there all along, she just wasn't seeing it. She was harboring sin and living in bondage and didn't even know it. The Holy Spirit revealed this in about five minutes, and she was free.

That is the very reason we must "Renew our minds daily by the reading of the Word" and have our quiet times before the Lord each day. Life is too big for us to handle otherwise. Most of the great people in the Bible have something terrific in common—they rose up early to be with the Lord. If you try that on, He'll catch you before the enemy does!

And the lady? She walked away feeling great. I saw her at a restaurant in a neighboring town a month later. She came running to me from across the dining hall and shouted, "I didn't think I'd ever see you again. Thank you, I mean thank Jesus...well, just look what He has done." She was completely straight—in body, soul, and spirit! No sickness at all. She could barely stand before, and now she was leaping! Her mother was with her and came to me weeping and praising God. Her husband said the miracle saved their marriage. He was ready to leave because of all the stress. Now she was just a jar of bubbles.

> *Beloved, I wish above all things that thou mayest prosper and be in health, even as thy soul prospereth. For I rejoiced greatly when the brethren came and testified of the truth that is in thee, even as thou walkest in the truth* (3 John 2-3).

Our souls prosper when we are honest with God and allow Him to reveal truth—not to put us into bondage, but to deliver us from it. Thank You, Lord, for the revelation of who You are, that destroys the revelation of who we are without you!

CHAPTER EIGHTEEN

New Destinations

I f we are willing, our journeys will lead us to a diverse variety of destinations and carry us to places that far exceed the "picture in the brochure." The Lord is after our willingness to obey at all costs. That was the heart of Christ as He pondered Calvary. That should be our heart as we ponder the hill we must climb to our resurrection victory. May we live in resurrection and not in the tomb!

When Lazarus was raised from the dead, the Pharisees wanted to kill him. He was no criminal—it was only after he was resurrected that they hated him. May you enjoy all that they attempt to do to you, knowing that you are alive in Him! Pray them through and consider the quest, which lays before you, worthy of walking for the glory of God.

As you go forward in the *Prayer of Job*, I pray that you will be inspired, motivated, and even ignited in Him. May we offer up more than He is asking for and shrink back from nothing, not even the attempt at perfection.

Blessings? Listen, you serve the Living God! He can't help Himself. He loves to bless His people. It's never been a matter of *if* He would bless you. It's a matter of, *will you let Him* bless you. He is always in full power position. As the Word says, "there is no shadow of turning with Him"—that's the high noon position on a sundial.

Trust Him to accomplish all that He has said He will. He is faithful, why wouldn't He be faithful to you? He is honorable, why wouldn't He honor you? He is loving, why wouldn't He love you? Moses didn't fully trust the Lord, so he grabbed Aaron. In the beginning of his journey, he trusted flesh more than God. Don't linger in your desert for 40 years. Pack up today and move on across the Canaan County line. Job's prayer will get you there.

The process by which Job learned to "see and not hear" was a strategic journey orchestrated by God Himself so that Job would know about fellowship. Fellowship cries for the heart of God. Fellowship cries out for the heart of its enemies: "Let them know you, God, and bless you at all costs—even at my cost." Sweet communion with the Lord comes by no other way. The Lord is a "rewarder of those who diligently seek Him." May we be as diligent as Job in speaking life into our enemies for the sake of the One we call Master and Friend.

Job had to remember who he had become as he approached the privilege to pray for his enemies. He also had to remember the good things that he was before, those things that God had perfected. But he had to be willing to move, not in the way he formerly did, but in the new way God had shown him. He had to remember the words his friends professed over him in the beginning, before they were defiled and before he was confused. For example, in Job 4:4 it is recorded that they told him, "Your words have supported those who have stumbled; you have strengthened faltering knees."

If it was true before in a shadow, would it be true now with the light shining upon him? Was he perfected or not? What did his trial do to him? As we watch his gift move toward maturity, we see a testimony of his ability to be made more perfect through trial. He must have found the words that his friends spoke and turned them into a prayer to seek abundance for them even though they were stumbling and faltering, and in spite of what they had put him through. He prayed because God's desire had finally become greater than his own. That desire was no longer vague, nor did it stem from tradition. It was clear as crystal. He was willing, above all else, to follow God's whisper, "Pray for them! Pray for them that they might be free and blessed, forgiven and whole."

When Job lost his blessings and greatness, he was faced with his relationship with God. How deep did it go? What was in the way of their fellowship? Could he trust God to be righteous in spite of his current reality? Sometimes our reality wars against our faith. Job lost it all to find it all.

His prayer released him from a captivity that he wasn't even convinced he had until tragedy hit. Job's prayer released his friends from their innermost bondage and brought healing. The willingness to pray that prayer is what the Lord has tried to impart to you throughout these pages. Be brave, my friend, He will not fail you. Live the life of the *Prayer of Job*, and He will live in your blessings, visiting them upon you with joy.

Your questions may have changed since you began this journey with Job. Before, you may have asked "Why?" and now you might be asking "How?" The secret that has helped me is found in Colossians.

> *Whatever you do, do it heartily, as unto the Lord and not unto men; knowing that of the Lord ye shall receive the reward of the inheritance, for ye serve the Lord Christ Jesus* (Col. 3:23-24).

Sometimes, it's too hard to do what Jesus would do; I

may not always understand what that is. After all, Jesus cleaned out the temple with a whip. Yes, righteously done; but in our deep desperation, sometimes, our causes seem just as righteous and we just want to grab a whip.

If we can attempt to be a true servant of Jesus Christ, then the *Prayer of Job* will come naturally. In serving others as a servant of Christ, we must believe that we are serving Him. The Lord said that "if you have done these things to the least of them, you have done it unto me." It's Jesus we are serving, not them.

The verse in Colossians says to do it "unto the Lord." In other words, pretend that you are doing it for Jesus. I have always tried to take it a step further (because I always needed the extra help) and actually imagine that the person I am serving (whether I want to or not) is Jesus. Doing for them as if they were Jesus puts an entirely different twist on things. It makes us more excellent, fervent, and diligent in what we are doing. We come to the place where we complain less and love more.

Let it be said that we seek to pray Job's prayer daily as we seek the truth of who Christ is and who He longs to be in each situation that surrounds us. The Holy Spirit will give us strength as we attempt to follow His lead in raw honesty and are guided down the path of freedom from our bondage. Job's heart must have soared as he prayed what we have learned:

The Prayer of Job

*Lord, there is nothing, there is no one
who compares to You. I humble myself before You.
Search my heart and expose every motive and fear that
hinders deeper fellowship with You. Help me to trust
You through difficult trials, for they open my eyes
and heart to see You as You really are! Lord,
as for those who have come against me,
I ask You to turn Your anger from
them, forgive them, and bless
them abundantly!*

May you have great success in all that He sets your
hands to do!

Testimonies
From

The following are testimonies received
from people whose lives have been forever
changed by *The Prayer of Job.*

Testimonies

"My husband died six months ago. Then my son was killed in an auto accident two months ago. Three weeks ago I was diagnosed with cancer. I thought I was pretty tough. I thought I had a lot of Jesus. I thought wrong. I was madly in love with my husband, and when he died, I was crushed but not destroyed. I maintained my strength for my son, who had lost his father. But, when my son died, I realized I had gotten my value from being a mother and a wife and not from Christ.

"A friend gave me your book, *The Prayer of Job*. I took an afternoon to read it, then an evening to read it again. Then the night hours compelled me to read it again. Morning came and I read it again. Now, I know the truth, 'Jesus IS the lifter of my head.' I just have to allow Him to get His hand on the back of my neck. Stiff necks don't allow that very well!

"The cancer is responding to treatments—'miraculously well' is how the doctor put it. But, that is not the real miracle. The real miracle and the reason for this note is, I want to thank the people responsible for getting this book out there. I could feel death inside me, and it is gone now. When my bad attitude toward God left, then so did that feeling of death. I *blamed* God for the loss of my husband, but I *hated* Him for the loss of my boy. Now, I see. God has them and He also has something wonderful for me to do here, without them, but WITH HIM!

"My joy has returned like a fresh spring day. I am no longer crying endlessly and in horror. I have no pain and am full of expectation. In your book, you said to dig deep. When I did, I found I hated God because I missed my family so very much. I was shocked to see what was in the 'cemetery

of my soul,' as you said, and I would like to thank you for causing me to not be afraid and dig that up. Thank you, thank you, thank you. Oh, the joy that fills my soul!"
—*Nila, California*

———

"I used to work for Satan in the Nevada mob. I hurt a lot of people and you wouldn't think a man like me would even want to read a book on prayer. But, I've had a praying mother, and I guess it caught up with me. I have come to understand the great and massive love of God because of your book, *The Prayer of Job*. Thanks for writing it. I know now that I can love Jesus because He loves me and no matter what, He is on my side.

"I have turned 'states evidence' because of *The Prayer of Job*. I have to do what is right now, I just have to. Well, I figure that I'll be going to prison for what I've done. That's okay because I'm taking three things with me: the Lord, the Bible, and *The Prayer of Job*. Could you please send a case to my mother? After I get locked up, she'll get me them so that I can share this life-word with the inmates. I promise not to *make* them read it, but be the new man that God created in me this week and *ask* them if they want to.

Maybe God will deliver me, but that's not the issue. The issue is my heart. I am truly forgiven and now I can forgive others. I never cared before, but now that I know how much the Lord loves me, I can't help but care. Thanks again for what you've done for me. And, I thank the Lord Jesus Christ for not forgetting about me."
—*Name Withheld, Nevada*

———

"For months, everything in my business was turning to dust. Each day brought another source of discouragement and failure. I have known the Lord for over 40 years, but never have I had my faith tested as it has been these past months.

"It was so refreshing to read your book, *The Prayer of Job*. I gained new insights to help me through the trials. I thought I had it all figured out, since I have even taught the book of Job to adults in the past.

"I have learned to trust Him more, and whenever I catch my soul getting scared over circumstances, I can tell my soul to back-off, and I am then able to allow my spirit the freedom to trust Him again."

—*Alan, California*

"*The Prayer of Job* saved my life and I just wanted you to know. I had heard about the story of Job before, as a Jehovah's Witness. I was raped by my mother's boyfriend 20 years ago, but she didn't believe me as a child and still doesn't now—even after he was arrested and put in jail for child molestation (of a neighbor child this year).

"Somehow, I recovered from my anger and hatred for her, after reading your book about Job. I found Jesus Christ as my personal Savior and forgave this man and my mother. But, when he was put in jail and she *still* didn't believe me, I can't tell you the depth of my pain. Then, because I had forsaken the ways of the Jehovah Witnesses, my entire family turned against me.

"I had become suicidal. I had made 3 attempts and failed. Now, I put the Prayer of Job on my refrigerator and pronounced it over myself and my mother every day. I remembered what I had learned through the Word of God and your book, and I made it through. I am completely set free today, and I no longer care if my mother believes me. I simply want to love her and watch Jesus bless her. That is the beautiful place that this 'giving' prayer brought me to. Then, just when I wasn't desperate for it anymore...

"Through this attitude of love and forgiveness, just this morning, my mother said she was sorry that she never believed me and that she just couldn't admit it because she couldn't carry that guilt. So she pretended that it never happened, and it was easier to believe it was a lie.

"I've been taking her to lunch once a week for 6 months and just loving her. The love of Jesus has spoken the truth to her louder than my pain or words. She has asked for my forgiveness, and I was in such joy to give it. We are restored, and my mother has even walked away from the Jehovah's Witness cult and now embraces this Jesus, blessed Savior whom I serve! My brothers and sisters have stopped persecuting me, and one has even committed to Christ along with many of my cousins!

"Yes, joy comes in the morning. I love this sunrise I am finally able to live! Thanks for saving our family through the love of God."

—*Dawn, Georgia*

"I am only 12 years old, but I hope you don't mind me writing to you. Us kids have things to deal with that parents don't have to. I have people every day telling me lies and calling me names. I don't think adults have people yelling names at them everyday. Kids do.

"My mom was reading your book and was crying. I asked her why she kept reading it if it was making her cry so much. She said because it was healing her, and it was just hard medicine to take, but it was right and good medicine. I could understand what she was saying with that medicine story. I don't like medicine very much, but after it's gone, I do feel better.

"I read your book about the man named Job after my mom was done. Mom was happier, so I thought this medicine would be good for me too. The coolest thing has happened. I used to have a lot of kids making fun of me and calling me names because I don't look quite right. But afterward I forgave them—I mean I totally and for sure forgave them! And then I started smiling at them and asking Jesus to bless them and forgive them each night like Jesus did, like in your book. I would go to bed at night and cry for their lives, instead of mine.

"Then in just two weeks, they all quit teasing me, and one girl has even shared her lunch with me and sometimes helps me get to class. I never had a friend before. I was just sorry for myself. But now, I have so much splendor in my life I just can't believe it. This was pretty good medicine—it worked in only two weeks. And, it's good for Jesus, because now my neighbor who used to hate me is gonna go to church with me this week.

"Thanks for being God's doctor down here, 'cause we need it—and a lot of it. Well, that's my story and I was in a writing mood, so I thought I'd let you know that this medicine is working over here in Arizona. I hope you get this letter so you can know it was worth it. Thanks for everything that you have done for me and my mom."
—*Alana, Arizona*

"I have been a homosexual for eleven years. I remember being molested by my uncle when I was five and ever since then, I remember wanting other men. I never said anything to anyone. I kept going to church and trying to stop my feelings, but I couldn't.

"Late last year, I started molesting my younger brother and cousin; then at church camp last month, I had an encounter with a homosexual man and everything was exposed because someone saw us. I guess I was grateful to

116

have it over with, but I couldn't get free. The director of the camp gave me your book, and because of the truth there, I've been able to pray the prayer of deliverance on myself, with the help of my parents, and forgiveness for my uncle. I actually want him blessed with salvation, and it makes me cry when I think of how good it will be for him to really know Jesus.

"I am free! Not only free, but everyone at church and school is rejoicing with me because my deliverance is so evident. They KNOW Jesus is real! They ask how I am, and I say, 'I AM A DELIVERED MAN!'

"Thanks a lot for forcing me to face my past and embrace my future. I pray for the wife and children that someday God will give me. Thanks a lot for going with Jesus and writing about Job."

—*Paul, California*

"We have been going through a legal battle that is based on false accusations. My husband lost his job and work equipment. We have been slandered in the town and may lose our home. This lie has spread to a bizarre level. I can't imagine that this could happen in the United States.

"We read your book, and boy-oh-boy did we ever get set free. We started to rejoice over our adversaries and began to see, through the eyes of the Lord, their pain and sorrow of life. My husband's old boss was the one who started all of this, and we have taken him to the Lord—not to be delivered of him, but to ask the Lord how we should pray for him. We began to weep over his life and really took a burden for him. That was 3 weeks ago. Today, we were told that all charges have been dropped."

—*Sonya, California*

"I guess you hear a lot of stories about pastors failing

lately. Well, here's another one for you. I suppose it's therapy for me to write it. I had a lot of excuses for why I did what I did. The truth is, I'm a pastor here in Mississippi, and there is no excuse. I destroyed my family and the family of the woman I had an affair with. I destroyed an entire church and a big piece of a community. I did this all because I had needs. I had needs that I didn't let the Lord tend to. I got my identity from ministry and not the Lord. You warned about this in the book, but I didn't listen. I read *The Prayer of Job* and refused to come alongside the truth in it. I was in love, not with the other woman, but with myself and all my clinging needs.

"My wife will have nothing to do with me. I don't blame her. She has divorced me, and my children hate me. The woman I had the affair with became pregnant and lost the baby. Her husband left her. She was always childless and when she became pregnant, she wanted this baby so bad. When she lost the baby, she said it was God's judgment upon her, and she too will have nothing to do with me now. It is only the Lord that remains.

"Alone with the Lord is where I should have found myself earlier, then I wouldn't be in this mess. I'm on the other side of *The Prayer of Job*. I have finally taken its elements and applied them to my life, and now I pray that those I have so miserably hurt and destroyed will be able to pray this prayer *for me*.

"Thanks for reminding me that Jesus will love me, no matter what I've done. I have repented and seek His face now, as there is nothing else to see of any great value— nothing outside of Christ. I am ashamed that it has taken me so long to come this way, but thank the Lord, the road was still open when I finally woke up!"

—*Name Withheld, Mississippi*

Testimonies

"My dad has been cantankerous forever. It is truly part of his personality. We love him, but he is what's called a 'hateful cuss' around here. Dad got cancer, and he fought it with all he had. He fought the cancer with anger and everyone around him as well. Then one day, he quit fighting and we got worried. Dad quit getting up and gave up. He quit shouting and he quit yelling. He quit snapping orders at everyone, and we couldn't figure it out.

"Two weeks ago today, I went in to see him and saw this book under his mattress. He forgot to shove it all the way in. It was *The Prayer of Job*. When he saw that I noticed the book, he grabbed for it, but I was quicker! I smiled with joy and then I began to laugh. I laughed so hard that he joined me! I never remember laughing with my dad before.

"I sat down and asked him to tell me about it. His face lit up with excitement. He sat up in bed and told me all about what you told him to do. He spoke as if he had a conversation with you! I asked him how he got your book and he won't tell me. That ornery streak is still there! He said that he began to read it and got mad. Then he got sorry, then he got emotional. Dad emotional? Well, he stayed in that room reading and repenting, he said, for almost a week. He found that Jesus goes beyond an idea, and he walks with Him now.

"He says that he has been prayin' for the Lord's broken heart over people who hurt Him, and he's been prayin' for people that he has hurt, and he's been prayin' for those who have hurt him. He says that he spent a lot of time prayin' for himself first because he figured he needed it most. He was right! Well, we are all just so thrilled to have dad so happy and full of Jesus, and we wanted to say thanks.

"Even the doctor said that there is proof that a joyful heart will heal quicker and respond to medicine better. So, we don't know if God will give dad a miracle and heal him, or He will use the doctor's hand to make Dad well, or if the Lord will take Dad home to be with Him. But, whatever happens, this is for sure, Dad will be tolerated in heaven now, and we won't have to lie at his funeral! There are so many wonderful things to say about Dad now, he has become a treasure!"

—*Nancy, Arkansas*

"I have read your book, *The Prayer of Job,* and I will tell you that I am expecting God to completely reveal Himself in a powerful way to the entire city through this revelation. It has been six months of studies that we have been doing so far out of this book, each and every Wednesday night. Much of our time, nowadays, is spent listening to testimonies.

"Each member of this group has been radically changed by this concept of asking forgiveness and praying a blessing on one who has done them harm. Parents are seeing their children come to Christ. Businesses, which were on the verge of closing, are gaining financial power. And the happiness is amazing. Happiness and joy are a gift. We here in India don't experience this gift too often in abundance. We have become a people of dismay that the enemy has been allowed to 'put upon.' He will only put upon us what we let him, and we have found that out through the study of your book in relation to the Word of God, our holy and precious Bible. The more we pray for those who are hurting us, the happier we become.

"Thank you for leaving these books here when you came to India; we are putting them to good use."

—*Pastor Bsori, India*

"I have been trying for nine years to get pregnant. Doctors can't explain it. I suppose it was like Hannah, where

120

God actually 'shut her womb.' So, I have lived this, praying for a baby, but mad at God. I didn't realize I was mad at God until I read your book. I didn't think it would hurt me like it did—it actually wrecked me. This was a good wreck though. Once I got rid of the anger and was able to seek forgiveness, then I began to pray for others and forget about praying for myself and my poor pathetic situation all the time.

"Guess what? I'm pregnant. We are going to name the baby Sandra and wanted you to know. We praise the Lord in all of this, but we thank you for being the voice that was not afraid to write a book that shouts at our hypocrisy. Blessing back to you."

—*Vivian, Indiana*

"I have lived a life that I'm not too proud of. I never thought that God could love me. Once, I almost believed Him, but the devil talked me out of it.

"I read your book that talks about Job's trouble, and I realized that I was afraid to love God. I was afraid that if I really tried to love God, I would have to feel more shame and condemnation for what I have done. If I didn't love Him, then I could pretend that He didn't notice the terrible things I'd been doing, the things I kept doing.

"So, your book says to dare to believe. I like a good challenge, so I began to ask God to show me His love, so that I could have the courage to believe that He would save and help me. He did. I am free!

"I am an African-American man, and I feel like I can relate to my forefathers now in a way that I never could before. When they were set free from slavery, great was the day!

"I too, am now set free from my slavery. My slavery from sin, hopelessness, and disbelief is completely gone. The

121

Word of God says that 'God will complete the work He has begun in me!'"
—*Charles, Missouri*

———•—•———

"Both my parents belonged to the brotherhood of Satan. I guess it's not something that people talk about, at least not in America. But it's real, and I wanted you to know that I read your book and it set me free. My parents were both killed by the brotherhood because they found Jesus through the love of a neighbor. They knew their end was coming and so they whisked me away to my aunt's house, who has a different name and lives in a different state. They prayed that I would not be found. I cannot say why they didn't have the faith to be spared themselves. I guess they knew that God had a plan greater than them staying here on this earth. Their prayers have been answered. I was never found and the commission that was set up to find me seems to have disintegrated.

"Why am I telling you all of this? Because I want you to understand, without graphic and horrible detail, the life I came from and the bondages that I faced. I was part of some of the rituals that my parents took part in when I was younger. In fact, I have memories from as early as I can remember until I was 15. That's when my parents found Jesus to be the true King and caused me to know the same. I must admit, though, I didn't understand that He actually had a heart and cared until I read your book.

"I have finally begun to pray for the people who killed my parents. The freedom that it brought me is unspeakable, that is, I cannot put it into words. My memories are faded, and I am walking in a purity I never even dreamed possible. I am 20 years old now and am going to Bible school. I don't speak of the past anymore, only the future. God has made it bright. Thank you for allowing me to know the power of a true prayer—the prayer that comes from God's heart Himself. The prayer that tells Satan that he cannot and will not win."

—Name Withheld, New York

"My wife died giving birth to my son. Then my son, Alex, died three years ago from leukemia, and I'm afraid although I didn't hate God for it, it had caused me to not be able to trust God any longer. Thanks for *The Prayer of Job*. Through its pages, the inspiration of the Holy Spirit, and the Word of God, I have finally come to understand that my God is trustworthy. Alex is with his sweet mother and Jesus. This is good enough for me.

"I'm afraid I can't put into words the relief and actual joy that has re-entered my heart after learning to trust Jesus again. I have missed Him so very much. I settled for *relationship* and missed that *fellowship* I once had. The book mentioned this, and it set me to crying for almost an hour. There was much redemption in those tears that night. I found the truth. I miss my Janine, yes, and Alex. But the pages of the book caused me to realize how much I missed my Lord too, for I had shut Him out. Thanks for bringing me home."

—Bill, Colorado

"I'm single and past 40. I've been bothered by that for a long time. I hadn't had a date for three years; no matter how hard I manipulated a situation! I read your book, and now I'm not bothered anymore. All I can do is thank the Lord for who He wants to be in me. I have fallen in love with the Lord and have no need for a man, only the Creator of man!

"Now, wouldn't you know it, I've got more dates than I care to! Oh, my Jesus has such a sense of humor. A year ago, I would have jumped at the chance to go out. Now, I don't really care about that. He will tell me what to do. It's hearing and knowing Him that I really care about. Thank you for pointing that out to me. Nothing is more important than Jesus or our pursuit of Him."

—*Rachel, Idaho*

———

"I am a pastor and have always had a weight problem. I have felt that it was such a bad witness to be 200 pounds overweight. But I just couldn't seem to lose it. I guess I never really tried that hard.

"I read your book. I must admit, I left it on the desk for a couple months before I got to it; but once I did, what an impact it had on my life and my entire congregation!

"Through the pages of *The Prayer of Job*, I have discovered the root of so many things that have been bugging me. There has been a distrust of the Holy Spirit in my life, which the Lord has helped me to remedy. I suppose He's still working on it, but I wanted to let you know that I have lost 100 pounds in nine months and I feel fantastic. My family and church are full of new faith and vigor. We have become an honest people. Keep provoking us to be honest with God. We are saints, but the human kind, we need all the help we can get!"

—*Dan, Montana*

———

"My wife left me for another man five years ago. I was never around, so I don't really blame her. Well, the reason I'm writing is because after reading your book and pondering the cost of obeying the principles in it for about a month—I went for it. I asked God to make me be 'that kind of Christian.' You know, the REAL kind. The kind that Jesus would be proud of, the kind that Calvary would shout 'well done' to. I looked at my own heart and mind and then forgave those around me. I don't know why, but this forgiveness was different than before. I actually couldn't wait to pray for my enemies every morning when I woke up. It became the biggest thrill for me. I could feel the Lord's heart rejoicing as I did it.

"My wife called last week—I should say ex-wife. She has left her third boyfriend since leaving me, got saved, and wanted to talk. We went out and I have absolutely no anger towards her at all. If I hadn't read your book, I would have told her to 'take a flying leap.' But I have so much love for her, I can't believe it. She is genuinely sorry for what she did and is truly a saved and beautiful creature of our Lord. We are going out on a date tonight, and I just wanted to thank the Lord for His faithfulness."

—*Dave, Alaska*

"After reading your book and praying that prayer, I put my bottle down and have never taken another drink. Thanks for giving me the courage to do that. I thank Jesus for His ability He put in me to fight fear with His own courage. I know that my children will have a better life because I am able to do all things through Christ and I intend to live that.

"My husband left a few years ago, and I guess I've been bitter about that. Well, I knew I really forgave him when I could speak a blessing over him. Thanks for showing me how. After that is when I had no more desire for alcohol. I am totally free of it. I've tried every program in the book, and they all failed. Jesus, however, never fails!"

—*Donna, California*

"I have been a thief for as long as I can remember. I have never gotten caught because I guess I was pretty good at it. I have a great job, but have always stolen from my employer. I always said that it wasn't hurting anyone, so who cares. I believed in God and Jesus. I read *The Prayer of Job* because a girlfriend wanted me to, and she kept talking about it. So, I read it to please her.

"I'm now going to church and have totally repented for what I have done. My girlfriend was always saved, but I was just faking it to get her. Now, I'm real. This is the most real thing that I have ever done. I have never known this kind of peace. It comes from being honest with God, my girlfriend says. She kept saying the Lord would teach me how, but I didn't believe her until I read that book. I'm now reading the Bible everyday and becoming the man of God that I was pretending to be.

"I work a lot of overtime at my job now, and never charge for it. I'm trying to find ways to pay back what I have taken. I want so badly to be a man of integrity and honesty now. Thanks for the lessons."

—*Michael, Pennsylvania*

- - - - -

"On my first wedding anniversary, my husband was killed by a drunk driver. I found out that week that I was pregnant. I went through it alone—both my parents died three years ago and I have no siblings. I never knew my husband's family; he was estranged from them, and they live 2,000 miles away.

"My daughter is three months old now, and I thought it was important that someone know the impact this book has had on my life. My daughter is a joy and I named her that, hoping to get my joy back. But, I found that Jesus is the only way to gain true and lasting joy!

"While waiting in line at the post office, I saw the book, *The Prayer of Job,* in the hands of someone. They seemed to be compelled somehow to read it. They were just standing there transfixed by it. I asked if it was good and told them I had always wondered about Job. This woman looked up with tears in her eyes and gave me the book. I tried not to take it, but she said she would get another one. She said she felt that I needed it. Boy, was she right.

"I went through the book like it was honey and I was a bear! Again and again I read it, and the truth that it revealed amazed me. I asked Jesus to come into my heart. I forgave those who killed my husband and then began to seek the blessing of salvation for them from the Lord. This is the greatest blessing I thought. I desired to pray the greatest of all blessings on them. Slowly, my heart began to feel joy. I am so happy now. When someone does something to hurt me, I immediately ask the Lord to forgive them and I begin to seek salvation and blessings for them.

"I went to the phone book and picked out a church in my neighborhood. God has given me a new family now in my church, and I'm involved with helping the community in so many ways. I often look for that lady who gave me the book that day, but cannot find her. I pray for her a lot, but maybe it's not necessary—maybe she was just an angel!

"Thanks for taking the time to write your book and to read this. My life is so full that I can hardly bear the goodness of it. My joy has returned and my baby Joy will grow up in a home full of happiness and truth."

—*Brenda, California*

"I have been lonely for a very long time. I am an immigrant from Poland and after being in this country for eleven years, my wife left me three years ago. I read your book and I will tell you that I discovered many evil things in my heart. Upon praying about them and dealing with them in the way the Lord asks us to, as written in *The Prayer of Job*, my heart became light and I found peace again in my life. I began to seek comfort from the Lord again, like I used to when my wife was with me, and my days are full of joy.

"Then the Lord did a most wonderful thing for me—just for me because He loves me. He brought me a very sweet and kind lady friend whom I enjoy spending time with very much. I have cleaned out my heart, and I thank you for helping me let Jesus do that."

—George, Oregon

"I have suffered physically for most of my life. Then, I got mad at God and suffered persecution. I was angry, bitter, and very disappointed. I had fibromyalgia, osteoarthritis, and a seriously weak liver; then I developed diabetes.

"I was too upset to read *The Prayer of Job*, so I refused to. Just a dumb book on prayer, I thought. Two of my family members' lives were turned around by the book. They were full of joy and peace. Everything, all of a sudden, seemed to be going their way. I read the book out of purely selfish motives. Once I began to read, almost immediately, the Holy Spirit revealed to me that I really didn't know Christ, that I had lost Him in my pain—instead of gaining Him there, as most people do. So, I repented and asked the Lord to come into my heart. It took me a good month to feel 'transformed.' I read *The Prayer of Job* seven times (I figured my walls were about the size of Jericho!) and then I finally 'got it.'

"I have been healed of the fibromyalgia and diabetes, and my liver is completely normal. My arthritis is getting better, but I have such a burden for the doctor who is treating me for that, I figure God is allowing it so that I will continue to pray for him. I rejoice in all things now and start each day with hope and great anticipation of blessing

God and others. And surprisingly in that, I am so very richly
blessed."
—*Keani, Alaska*

"My daughter died in a boating accident five years ago. I
have four boys who are wonderful, but she was my only girl.
Sweet and gentle at six years old, and she was my joy. In
fact, Maryanne was everyone's joy.

"I have carried guilt and horrible pain because this accident was my fault. I didn't cause the accident on purpose, but
I wasn't being as careful as I should have been and I knew
better than to drive recklessly with the children in the boat.
My wife had told me to slow down...if I had only listened.

"The reason for the letter to you is that ever since that
day I haven't had any joy. Not a bit. I don't know why my
wife has stayed with me. Probably because she loves the
Lord so much and maybe because she felt sorry for me.
Well, I read your book and I feel compelled to tell you of the
impact it has had on me and my family.

"I was finally able to let go of the guilt. My poor boys
haven't had a dad since the accident, and little Norman feels
the weight of guilt as well because Maryanne was helping
him with his life jacket when her life was taken. He is also
free of pain and guilt because of the instruction in this book.
My marriage has been renewed and I can finally hope in
Christ once more. Even though my memories of that day
are vivid, I have new memories now. I am finally able to see
Maryanne in heaven with the Lord, happily waiting for us,
playing with other children there, being taught by the angels, and loving Jesus. I have my life back. Thanks. And,
thanks be to God."
—*Jack, California*

"I'm not ashamed to say that I have been a prostitute. I'm not ashamed of it because I'm totally forgiven of it. Your book about Job made me know that there was hope for me. A preacher was walking around in my district. Those guys usually hand out tracts, but this guy was handing out your book. I can't explain it, but it made me feel human again. A book—nobody had ever given me a book! So, trying to be noble, I read it. In six hours, my life was different.

"I have found a church and I've moved away from my trouble. I have forgiven and blessed as instructed in the book, and God ran to me when I did. I'm free—thanks for that. I thank Jesus each and every week that you wrote that book and that the man gave it to me, I've never seen him since, although I tried to find him. Well, as pastor says, maybe he was just an angel! Maybe you are too!"

—*Jane, California*

"*The Prayer of Job* was left on an airplane for me by God. It's as clear as that! I assume the person who read it was impacted enough to want to share it. The cover compelled me to look at it, so I did.

"After three divorces and seven children, I finally found out the truth. From the Introduction, the book had me. I had a four-hour flight and finished the book when we landed. All I can say is, 'Thank you.' My heart has peace and is light for the first time in my life. I've tried to live the Christian life but was unable to. Now I know why.

"I was molested as a kid and have had anger for many years because of that. Your book pulled that hatred out of me and today I plan on going to the one who caused me this pain, embrace him in the name of Jesus, and forgive him. I am so excited to forgive, I can't even believe it. I will spend this week, taking time with my ex-wives. I'm gonna get them all in a room and make it an all-day confession and repentance time. I hope they let me. My children? Oh, I can be a father now. Thank you so much to the lady who wrote this. I have been found."

—*John, Ohio*

"I was raped as a young girl and became pregnant. Then I married a man and had three more children. He was abusive and ended up going to prison and eventually was murdered there.

"Next I married a wonderful Christian man. However, it turns out that he had a pornography problem that led him into a perversion that I don't think he ever wanted to embrace. He began to molest my children, one by one. The lies of the enemy caused my children to believe that I would be harmed if they told on him, so out of their love for me, they kept their silence. Then one day it all came out. One of my daughters confessed it to me and I confronted him. He admitted it and today is in jail.

"Time and the love of the Lord was healing my family when I came to realize my love for a widowed man in our church. He was truly full of Christ upon this earth. I haven't always been a good judge of character, so I let my children choose for me! They said he was a perfect man and they were right. We had two of the most beautiful years of my life. This man put our family back together with the love of God and then he got cancer. The struggles that we went through were unbelievable. They went on for over a year and just ended a few months ago. My husband has gone on with Jesus into glory.

"During my husband's illness, a friend came in and gave me *The Prayer of Job* while I was at the hospital. I had no desire at all to read this book, so it sat there for a few weeks.

131

The complications from his cancer and surgeries were unbelievable. I was endlessly at the hospital and one day my husband asked me to please read *The Prayer of Job*. I would deny him nothing. At page one we both began to cry. It took us several days to get through the book because of our weeping. I came to realize that I had been desperate for the promises of God and not desperate for God. I was scared of what might happen to my husband, my perfect man. Instead I should have been concentrating on my perfect Lord. I couldn't trust God. I just couldn't.

"When the book says to 'lay the promises down and trust Jesus to perform them in His time,' my body began to shake. I realized I was worshipping hope and fear. When I got rid of that, I began to sleep at night. I began to sing again and I began to know that whatever happened with my husband, it would be okay.

"I had wanted him to live, but when he died it was all right because I knew I was trusting Jesus and not a man or a marriage. My children have seen a strength in me that I never had before, and it has inspired their faith. I can only imagine what would have happened to us all had I not read *The Prayer of Job*. It was especially wonderful to me that my husband and I went through the book together; we discovered so much truth together. I have grown to treasure that time as one of the greatest memories of my marriage. Thank you for that.

"Because God allowed my path to cross with a man who only had a short number of days left, my life has been abundantly enriched. I wouldn't trade those few short years in for anything, and I find myself grateful to this God whom I was mad at for so very long!"

—*Name Withheld, West Virginia*

Testimonies

"My 18-year-old daughter left home to move in with a 23-year-old man who has been beating her up. I wanted to kill the man. But my wife read *The Prayer of Job* and forced me to listen to her while she read. I fought it all the way.

"My daughter would come home from time to time all bloodied up and swear she wouldn't go back to him, and then after a couple days, she always went back. I was about to disown her when the heart of God spoke to me through *The Prayer of Job.*

"I realized that everyone around me also hated this man, and I wasn't helping the situation. My wife and I had a meeting with everyone and told them we intended to forgive this man as true Christians should do and then we were going to start praying for him and speaking the blessing of salvation over his life. So, we got started. Things got worse for a few weeks with my daughter; she was even rushed to the hospital once, and her boyfriend was almost out of his mind with drugs. We kept on praying and holding on for the truths that were released to us out of this book and through the Word of God.

"Then it happened almost all at once. He came to the house with our daughter. Said that he was sorry and that he wanted to find God. He delivered her to us like a beautiful package on Christmas. It was as if he was blind before and now he could see. I've never seen a man more repentant.

"It turns out he had a very abusive and terrible life without any love. Then when we weren't showing him the love of God, it confirmed to him that there was no God. But when we began praying for him and blessing him and actually doing nice things for him, it was a real testimony to him and he wanted what we had—Jesus!

"He is in church now and our daughter is living at home with us; we are all totally restored. Before I read that book,

133

the only way that this problem would have been solved is by somebody going to prison for murder. So, thank You, Jesus, for freedom. We are so blessed and I thought someone should know."

—Jerry, Indiana

"When I started reading this book, *The Prayer of Job*, I had bone cancer and was, as they say, 'on the way out.' Now my soul is full of revelation and revolution. My cancer is totally in remission. 'I shall not die, but live and declare the works of the Lord!' (Psalm 118:17)

"Each day after reading this book, the Lord revealed to me another truth about the 'cemetery of my soul' as you said. After a two week period of crying out to God, not for my own life anymore, but for the lives of those around me in brokenness, thank You, Lord, I began to notice that I had more energy than I had ever had before while being sick with the cancer. Each and every day, it seemed that the more I blessed others, the better I felt. The more I praised the Lord in all things, the better I felt. I guess I just blessed others, judged myself, and praised the Lord all the way to health! Hallelujah I am healed!

"The report is good from the doctor and outstanding from God. The cancer they say 'seems to have taken a break.' It's gone! Praise God!"

—Betty, Indiana

"My mother died of diabetes, as well as my aunt and my sister. I have had diabetes for 15 years, and it didn't look good. I read *The Prayer of Job* and God has totally set me free from fear and anger. My diabetes is gone, and I can hardly believe it. I keep going back to the doctor because I can't quite get a grasp on it.

Testimonies

"My husband and I were reading this book as an evening devotional before going to bed each night, and it slowly transformed us. We usually went to bed crying, if not for you, then for us, and if not for us, then the Lord Himself! At the end of the book, we prayed this prayer in awe of God and watched our lives be transformed, starting with our hearts! Our marriage has been elevated to a new and beautiful place, we are so very grateful. Diabetes has been a part of our family forever. I never expected to be rid of it. I just wanted to be closer to Jesus, I just wanted to learn to trust Him more.

"Then one day, I felt powerfully, wonderfully different. I went to the doctor to have some tests, and they said the diabetes had disappeared. I haven't taken my insulin shot for a month and I feel fantastic! My girlfriend told me that I ought to write to tell you what your efforts and the power of God has done for me, so here I am, writing to a complete stranger about the glory of God!"

—*Carol, California*

"Our ladies group at church has used *The Prayer of Job* for our text this quarter. At the end, we each proceeded to pray this prayer and ask God to reveal truth to us.

"I have had arthritis and a blood disorder for many years and have suffered much pain. When it came my turn to pray, I felt fire all over my body and a warm sense of peace. It was the power of God all over me.

"I am now completely healed from that moment a month ago. Completely healed! What a fantastic day and a fantastic book! What a fantastic God we serve."

—*Marly, California*

"We have been childless for nine years. We read your

book and now I am pregnant! We both had issues of distrust with the Lord and anger toward others. This combined with a fear of completely obeying God, made us perfect candidates to pray the Prayer of Job.

"We feel so light and free, clean and pure. We just feel so good and close to the Father. We feel like there is finally nothing in the way—we're a clean slate for Him to write upon. And, the first thing He chose to write was PREGNANT WITH CHILD! The word says that our sin builds a wall between us and God. Down with the walls! It's as if the womb was purposefully shut by God because of sin and with that gone...wham, clear sailing from here. Thanks!"

—*Andrew and Katie, Kansas*

"My wife got cancer and I lost my job all in the same week. Wow, there was never a more true statement made than when it is spoken in the book, 'The word of God came to try Job.' So, we followed the instructions in the book about trusting Jesus and in just a few short days, we were laughing all the way to the doctor. Our trials became a blessing to us! We could almost hear the devil throwing a temper tantrum. I never knew there could be so much excitement in the middle of tragedy. We never saw the tragedy, we always kept our eyes on the deliverance that was coming. Every day started with a true anticipation and excitement about what the Lord would do next. I have never felt so cared for or excited in my life, it was a wonderful experience to walk with the Lord through all of this. Today my wife is cancer free and how great it is to absolutely trust God like this, we never thought this life was possible.

"The very day money was almost out, I was offered a job. I'll be making more money and working less hours than before. We are a grateful family and the best part of all is our

136

children have seen this. Now they have a first hand experience of how a Christian should endure a trial—trusting Jesus. Thanks for letting us give them that heritage. Praise the Lord whom I serve with joy unspeakable and full of glory!"

—*Gary, California*

"My husband has committed adultery four times and I have stayed with him because I don't want my children to suffer. It has put a pain in me that I cannot explain. I have loved Jesus since I was small and counted on Him for many hard things. He has always been faithful. But this last infidelity has brought me to a pain I can't describe. Why wouldn't God intervene? 'I trusted You with my marriage and You failed me,' I screamed at Him.

"Empty and worthless. That's how I felt. I knew I would find my way back to God somehow, but in what condition? A friend of mine gave me *The Prayer of Job* and I threw it at her. I yelled, 'Why pray a prayer to a God that doesn't hear. He didn't hear Job and He won't hear me.' I have a forceful friend who, thank God, wouldn't walk away from me or my anger. She hugged me and as I cried, she wrapped her arms, the arms of the Lord around me. She made lunch for me out of the meager fare in my fridge and asked me to sit for 20 minutes while she read to me this book about Job and His prayer. She has been such a good friend to me, so out of respect, I agreed but asked her to limit it to 20 minutes. After five minutes, she had to stop because I was weeping so hard. We spent the rest of that day reading that book.

"I'll spare you a five-page testimonial of all the details, but know this: By the end of the day, I saw my husband as Christ did and was weeping for his soul. My friend and I decided that we would fast that week and pray the Prayer of

Job for my husband. I have never had such freedom or expectancy in prayer in my life. That next Sunday my husband not only went to church with me, but he gave his heart to the Lord, and now he is actually leading our family to a place of prosperity in the spirit and in this life. My anger was actually preventing his salvation.

"He has wept such bitter tears before me and before the Lord for what he did to me, but his heart is more broken for what he did to the Lord, which is actually comforting to me. He apologized over and over again to me. He is different. He never had such pain and regret for his sins before. He is like Peter weeping those hard tears after denying Christ.

"This man is reading his Bible instead of eating lunch. He said he is going to be fasting lunch everyday until the end of the year. He is in construction and I know it will be hard for him, but the effort he is making is causing me to fall in love with him all over again. It is only the Lord that can compel him to be so changed. I'm still amazed on Sunday mornings when my husband serves me breakfast in bed, declaring what a beauty I am and helping me get the kids ready for church. I believe that when he fell in love with Jesus, he fell in love with me all over again as well! Jesus has done a great thing here and it all started with a book I threw across the room!"

—*Sasha, California*

"I started a Bible study at work. First it was just three of us before work. Then it grew to 5 and 10. Now there are 34 of us that meet twice a week 45 minutes before work to study and share. The study guide has been very helpful. We are going to have to split the group because it's getting too big now and there is not enough sharing time before work starts!

"Please understand that all of these people who are in this Prayer of Job study (except the original three) were not saved before they started coming. They started coming because they heard our weekly testimonies around the office about the great things God was doing as we embraced the chapters and instructions in this book. My co-workers saw a change in us and then they wanted what we had. I suppose we were compromising Christians before, with little to offer, but now the group is 'the thing to do and the place to be!' Lives are being put back together because we are getting real with God. Thanks for shaking us up over here! My supervisor even allows us to play Christian music now at work! Just thought you'd like to know why I keep ordering more and more books!"

—*Gena, Florida*

"I learned through reading this book several times that Jesus is big enough to handle all that we go through and He is bigger than our problems. I have 8 children all under the age of 15 from three different men. My current husband is father to my last two. Before their birth I found the Lord but my husband did not care to be a Christian. He was still embracing our past lifestyle of anger, drunkenness and drugs.

"Within months of reading your book, all my children were saved, including my teenage daughter who was deep in rebellion. Before I lay them down at night, we pray the Prayer of Job, quite specifically over people that crossed their path that day. They each have become quite an example of God's overcoming ability and love.

"My husband just kept getting angrier and angrier. Last month, he hit my daughter very badly and for no apparent reason. I tried to stop him; he hit me and then he left. I determined to call the police and get him out of the house once and for all.

"My children came to me and asked if we could just pray for him one more time. Remember, these are children who have been abused by this man and most of them aren't even his natural children.

"We prayed for him, we prayed the Prayer of Job and reminded the devil that he had no business in our home. My children began to weep for my husband. They began to ask God to heal the wounds from his past that makes him so angry. They began to tell Jesus that they would love my husband no matter what.

"I don't know why we didn't hear him. Maybe it was all the crying. He normally makes a lot of noise when he enters a room, but not this time. After awhile, we heard him crying. He was sitting on the couch behind us, being held in the arms of Jesus. The children ran to him and my daughter called him 'Daddy' and said that she loved him. He begged her forgiveness and asked all the children to forgive him, including me. He found Jesus that day.

"No matter how long you wait for something, when the answer comes, it almost seems like it happened in an instant. This has been a miracle bigger than fire coming down from heaven. I still can hardly believe it and ask sometimes, 'Where's that man I married?' I am glad that he has been replaced by this godly man. He devours the Word and has made friends at church. He actually helps me around the house and is working full time. One of his greatest joys are the children and he is always finding something wonderful to do for them. He has been completely delivered of drugs and alcohol.

"When he asked me how I was able to hang on and wait for him, and how the children and I could forgive him, I gave him *The Prayer of Job*. He now understands the love of God that motivated us in our little family prayer meeting the day I was going to throw him in jail.

140

"His angry bones have disintegrated. The 'old man' is surely dead. I know it seems impossible, but he is a completely different man. It is a true miracle. It was my husband who asked me to write someone and tell them our great story because of God in *The Prayer of Job*. Thank you for provoking us to hang on just one more day, because one more day is all it took!"
—*Elaine, California*

———

"I had to write to you, I just had to! I don't know who will get this, but to God be the glory. I have been praying for my four sons for 20 years for them to be saved. I was saved late in life, so unfortunately they are living the life I used to live. But in the one year since reading and praying the Prayer of Job, all four of my sons have come to know the Lord Jesus.

"I have been angry for many years and didn't realize that anger was actually preventing my sons from finding Jesus because it was preventing my prayers from being heard. My anger took up all the room in my heart, so there was no room left to trust the Lord. When the anger left, the trust came and with it, a huge peace and now redemption of my sons. Thank you, Jesus! I shudder to think of the state of my heart and lack of trust that I had just a year ago. With the Lord's help, I will maintain this walk."
—*Iris, New York*

———

"I was a pretty miserable person until I found Jesus. When I found Him, I just wanted to sit at His feet and be loved on. I've had one of those lives of abuse and horror, and I just wanted to have someone love me without an agenda. *The Prayer of Job* explained to me that Christianity is more than that. Because of this book, I've been able to quit feeling

sorry for myself and start praying for other people. It is such a joy to pray for others. I could never do it when I was feeling bad for little old me all the time. I feel like I'm finally on the team."
—*Allison, California*

———————

"I have been a homosexual for 17 years. I could never really say how I got there before, but I know now. Some say that we are born this way. They are wrong. I always felt that I was in error somehow, but hadn't been able to get to the bottom of it until I read *The Prayer of Job*. I saw this book in the doctor's office of all places and the cover intrigued me, so I picked it up and asked if I could take it home for a few days and bring it back later.

"Through the pages of this book I have found God, and I thought I should tell somebody. You said that there is no sin that is bigger than Jesus, and I believe you. I have cut myself off from my gay lifestyle. I have this great and perfect peace.

"Praying the Prayer of Job has made me look into my face and discover things from my childhood that I didn't want to face. I was molested as a boy by another boy and then later by a man. It created in me this need for men and a false rejection of women. I gained my value from the gay lifestyle instead of the true identity that Christ had planned for me to have—the identity of being a child of God. I haven't had a stitch of therapy, it has all been Jesus over this past year, and I can honestly say I am no longer a homosexual. I have been totally set free by the power of Christ.

"Now I have a job that I love and a girlfriend that I love. We go to church together for every event and belong to a Bible study group. I never knew that life could be so good. I can hardly believe what God did in one short year, starting with a prayer coming from a trembling, hurting man trying to relate to Job (who I never heard of before) in order to find a Savior."

—*Arthur, California*

"I have had Lupus for seven years and a co-worker brought me *The Prayer of Job* to read. Oh, the joy that filled my soul to discover the power in this book. I'm a Christian woman, but nevertheless, human. So there were things hidden deep within my soul of not truly trusting God and wanting my own way. Praise the name of Jesus, He has shown me through these pages how to lay down my control and fear and how to totally trust Him. I read the book three times and really began to understand all the deep truths there.

"My Lupus is now gone. It seemed to disintegrate when my lack of trust left. It was as if my fear was holding that disease onto me. I have no symptoms at all, and the doctor says my blood levels are totally normal along with everything else. I am living proof of God's healing power. Thank you and God bless."

—*Evangeline, California*

"I was raped at the age of 12 by my father. I had an affair with a married man at 14 and at 17 became pregnant by my boyfriend who was killed of a drug overdose two months before my baby was born. My own mother told me that I was unwanted and my brothers and sisters who are much older than I am, made it clear I am not their type of person and don't want me around. When I told my mom what my dad did, she threw me out and I landed in a shelter. A lady who comes to the homeless shelter gave me a copy of this book two months ago, and she said I should write to you.

"I guess I hated everybody, especially God. I thought He could have done something to help me but chose not to. After I read this book I began to think a lot and ask the lady who gave it to me a lot of questions about Job, his prayer, Jesus' teaching, and also about my life and heart. I accepted Christ after reading this book and then I started to apply the principles in my life. I didn't want my baby to grow up mad at everybody like I did, so I gave the Lord and this prayer a chance.

"With much shaking and trembling, I began to pray this prayer and ask Jesus to help me. After about a month, my sister came to the shelter to talk with me. She hugged me and started to cry. I never experienced anything like this before. She said that she had stayed away from me because I reminded her of what happened to her (Dad molested her too) and what her life would have turned out like if she hadn't met her husband who rescued her. So then I cried because I had been praying for her but actually wasn't sure if my prayers coming from such a weak heart as mine actually got through. They did!

"She took me out of that shelter. Her and her husband have asked me to live with them. They watch my baby while I study to take my high school test. Their kids are grown, and they have the room and make me feel so glad to be here. I volunteer at the shelter now one day a week.

"I have a home and a heart now. Thanks for letting me trade my anger in for hope."
—*Debbie, Kentucky*

"Praise the Lord. Over the last ten years life has been tough for me. I have had failed businesses, failed relationships, and a failed ministry which eventually resulted in a failed faith. It seemed the more I trusted in the Lord, the more I got disappointed and heartbroken. I felt the Lord had forgotten about me and didn't care. When I prayed for something, the opposite would happen, so I lost the desire to take my requests to Him. I could not backslide—I have been saved for too long. I didn't know where to start in the world of non-believers and I knew better than to try. My attitude was: So here I am saved, but with nothing much to show for it. My only hope was that someday I would not suffer eternal flames.

"It's in this miserable situation that I read *The Prayer of Job*. I realized my problem was that I had wounded faith and that there was healing for my situation. My prayer life is now all healed, and I can bring all my cares before God, knowing that He is listening and cares about those things that seem to give me a hard time. I forgave others, I forgave God, and then I forgave myself.

"Suddenly some of the situations I had been praying about for years were answered. Opportunities are swinging open before me, and I'm also becoming a more pleasant person. Because the healing in my heart is so real, I can actually bring healing to other people now. God has just unleashed an anointing for me to be a blessing and a comforter to those who are facing situations that are destroying their faith."

—*Veronicah, Nigeria*

"I had always lived my life for myself. I was raised with money and was taught that the people who didn't have money were ignorant or lazy. I grew very judgmental of people who didn't have any 'means.' I married a selfish wife and we raised selfish children. Then my granddaughter was born retarded. I hated my son-in-law and blamed him for his 'bad genes.' I grew estranged from my daughter and her family. I couldn't stand the seeming lack in my grand-daughter, a 'defect' that I could not tolerate. I ignored my daughter's family and tried to pretend they didn't exist.

"Soon, my daughter and her side of the family had no use for me either. They moved away and soon afterward my wife died. I was determined to find a younger version of my wife and keep moving on.

"I still can't believe that I allowed my judgmental and critical self to rob me, even for a few short years, of my precious daughter and her family. The gifts of God that I threw away. My love for myself and my ideals had become larger than my love for anyone else.

"I lived in Arizona and my daughter had moved to Illinois. She read this book called *The Prayer of Job* and called me after not speaking to me for almost 5 years. She told me that she was flying out to see me and she did. There was something different about her. The lines of dismay and anger toward me were gone. She embraced me like I had never hurt her. She hugged me as if she was glad to see me. Her actions toward me broke me in half and totally humbled me. I had never had that happen before. I can't explain it, but it made we want what she had…desperately.

"She began to tell me how she read this book and it rekindled her walk with Jesus and how she needed to make things right between us, whether I wanted it or not. She had absolute raging love toward the Lord and was forcing me to partake of it. She forgave me and I forgave her. I cried and received the Lord into my life that day with my daughter's help. We flew to Illinois together and I saw my grand-daughter for the first time just a few months ago. I stayed for three weeks and drank in her joy. I am in love with my granddaughter now and am in the process of selling my home in Arizona to move to Illinois to be near her.

Testimonies

"All was lost, and then my daughter decided to fly to Arizona and insist on forgiveness. Thank you for giving me back my family. We are praying the Prayer of Job over my sons and expect great and mighty things in their lives as well.

"My heart is so light and my spirit so full, I just had to write and let somebody know that this prayer of forgiveness has worked wonders in my family. I give the Lord Jesus Christ all the praise for these things."

—*Alex, Soon to be from Illinois*

———•—•———

"I'm writing because I was a local church hypocrite and gossiper. I might as well have been a rapist and murderer, the way I feel about it now. I read your book and thought it was okay, but it wasn't really getting through, so I put it down.

"Then, our church's weekly ladies Bible Study started doing a study out of *The Prayer of Job*. I thought, 'Great, the dumb book.' I had to be gracious and act excited, so I did. Hypocrites can do that! I hosted it in my home (so I could act spiritual, I suppose) and someone else taught it.

"We got to the part where that man walked out of his wheelchair and I started shouting that it couldn't have been God. He wouldn't do that. Then they read the part about how mad the other church members got when that happened—how horribly hypocritical it showed them to be. I was fuming. Then I said that the guy probably wasn't even sick, he was an actor or something. Suddenly one woman said that she was AT that meeting and the man was her brother. He had been in that wheelchair for years! She was the one who got the book, because she has been following your ministry on the internet and attends whenever you are within 100 miles of her house.

"What was there left to do? I had to repent and ask for-

147

giveness from my sisters and from the Lord. So, now you
have a letter from a former hypocrite! Thanks so much for
letting me hate you for awhile, so that I could love so much!
I have never really known Jesus before. Never. We had a
Revival that day in my house and I pray the reality of God's
heart in your book continues to reveal constant truth to me.
My marriage and family have finally become stable. My son,
who ran away from home and was wandering the streets of
Los Angeles, has come home, my husband has been pro-
moted in his job, and me, I cry a lot! Thanks again for giving
me back my life—the life Christ intended for me to have."
—*Gloria, California*

"We are in Belize, Central America. I walk three miles to
the prison every day to help with the prisoners. Sometimes I
simply visit with them, other times I preach or counsel. It is
my volunteer position. Many of the men have received and
renewed their walk with the Lord Jesus Christ because of
The Prayer of Job. Even the man who was 'running' his cell
block has been converted to Christ. He now insists that
every man in his block sit in for the Bible study we do each
week out of the book. They come in angry and leave with
peace. These men are slowly learning how to trust Jesus,
something they have never done before.

"We will be turning out profitable citizens into the so-
ciety of Central America now. This book has been approved
by our government to be read in the prisons because of the
impact it was having in the small study groups I was doing.
So I thank you for your help with our reformation here.
Christian music is now playing in the men's prison 18 hours
a day over the loudspeaker.

"Our *Prayer of Job* study groups have increased by pop-
ular demand to twice a week. The prisoners 'police' each
other and threaten to beat the ones up who don't come to

the 'Job group.' They are still learning patience and love, but their hearts are getting right!"
—*Roy, Central America*

"We have translated *The Prayer of Job* into the Burmese language and through it many Buddhists are receiving Christ. I have taught this book as part of our curriculum at the Bible school here and many lives have been impacted. I thank you for this great tool for the Kingdom of God."
—*Brother Kap, Myanamar*

"I read *The Prayer of Job* on an airplane. I began to weep in the Introduction. Being a grown man, I felt odd about it, but I guess I was fed up up with my hard heart and all my pain, so I decided to let it go. My wife had left me and my children two years earlier. My pain over it was greater than I can say and my hatred was greater than I knew, and they were getting greater with each passing day. This book rooted it all up and I am finally free. My life doesn't revolve around what she did or what she is doing any longer, it revolves around Christ.

"My children and I pray for her every day at bedtime, and we also pray for her boyfriend. This has been a true testimony of forgiveness for my children. Instead of being mad at their mommy, they now pray for her and wish good things for her and her boyfriend. We are confident that through this prayer the Lord's will is going to be accomplished. My children already cry a lot less and happiness has returned to our home. My heart is ready for what God has next, and I am finally able to trust Him to bring it. Thank you for the insights that have so powerfully impacted my life."
—*Marvin, Tennessee*

ABOUT THE AUTHOR

Sandra Querin was called at the age of nine to "prepare for the day" when she would preach the Good News. Although hampered by cystic fibrosis for 30 years, she pursued her education while working. She holds a master's degree in business and a doctorate in law. Miraculously healed of her disease, she resigned her position as a college professor and became an ordained minister. She now travels through the U.S. and abroad, impacting communities with the Gospel. She has worked with Teen Challenge, YWAM, the Assemblies of God, Church of God, Baptist, Mennonite, Catholic, and Foursquare churches, among others. Untold numbers of salvations and miracles have been the result of her ministry. She has been married for 25 years and has two grown children.

To contact the author for
speaking engagements or ministry, write:

Sandra Querin • Abba's Heart Ministries, Inc.
P.O. Box 734 • Kingsburg, CA 93631
E-mail: abbasheart@abbasheart.com
Website: www.abbasheart.com
